QUESTIONS THAT MATTER

*Christian Answers
That May Surprise*

Barry L. Callen

Emeth Press
www.emethpress.com

QUESTIONS THAT MATTER: *Christian Answers That May Surprise*

Copyright © 2025 Barry L. Callen
Printed in the United States of America on acid-free paper

All rights reserved. No part of this book may be reproduced, or stored in a retrieval system or transmitted in any form or by any means, electronic, mechanical, photocopying, recording, scanning or otherwise, except as permitted by the 1976 United States Copyright Act, or with the prior written permission of Emeth Press. Requests for permission should be addressed to: Emeth Press, P. O. Box 533, Jackson, Georgia 30233.   http://www.emethpress.com.

Library of Congress Cataloging-in-Publication Data

Names: Callen, Barry L. author
Title: Questions that matter : Christian answers that may surprise / Barry L Callen.
Description: Jackson, Georgia : Emeth Press, [2025] | Summary: "You'd think the Bible of all books would be the one volume of assured final answers. Well, it is and it isn't. It seems to leave unanswered as many questions answers clearly. At least it orients our questions properly, answers the biggest ones, and assures us that life can proceed without all questions answered, at least for now.. This book addresses thirty-three of the really important faith-related questions that trouble people who think at all"-- Provided by publisher.
Identifiers: LCCN 2025028497 (print) | LCCN 2025028498 (ebook) | ISBN 9781609472146 paperback | ISBN 9781609472153 kindle edition
Subjects: LCSH: Christianity--Miscellanea | LCGFT: Trivia and miscellanea
Classification: LCC BR121.3 .C35 2025 (print) | LCC BR121.3 (ebook) | DDC 230--dc23/eng/20250828
LC record available at https://lccn.loc.gov/2025028497
LC ebook record available at https://lccn.loc.gov/2025028498

CONTENTS

                                                                        Page

Preface……………………………………………… v

A. THE GOD WHO IS

    1. How Smart Are We? LIMITED ……………… 1
    2. Can You Live with Mystery? DARE ………… 7
    3. Is God One or Three? YES ………………… 13
    4. Is God Weak? IN A WAY …………………… 19
    5. Should We Panic at Paradox? RELAX ……… 25
    6. Who Runs this World? BOTH ……………… 31
    7. Why Is Evil in the World? FREEDOM ……… 37
    8. How About a Good Idol? TYPICAL ………… 43
    9. Can You See the Star? ESSENTIAL ………… 49

B. THE LIFE THAT CAN BE

    10. Want To Be "Radical"? CAREFUL …………… 55
    11. Living a "YES" Life? ABSOLUTELY ………… 61
    12. Go with Nothing? RISKY …………………… 67
    13. What Does "Holy" Look Like? LOVE ……… 73
    14. Should Some Shut Up? YES ………………… 79
    15. Beyond *Quid Pro Quo*? DEFINITELY ……… 85
    16. How Can We Be United? BE HOLY ………… 91
    17. Why Write Your Life Story? WITNESS …… 97

C. THE CHURCH THAT OUGHT TO BE

    18. Call Me "Christian"? NO …………………… 103

19. Which Is the Real Church? NONE 109

20. Who's In and Who's Out? DEPENDS 115

21. Why Read the Bible? DON'T 121

22. Read the Whole Bible? NO 127

23. Which Church Music? DIVERSE 133

24. Both Christian and Patriot? DIFFICULT 139

25. Is There a Hole in the Roof? NO DOUBT ... 145

26. When There Are No Rules? LOVE 151

27. The Church's Future? GUIDELINES 157

D. THE FUTURE THAT WILL BE

28. If God Doesn't Answer? STAY ANCHORED.. 163

29. The Best Way to Die? DON'T 169

30. Are These the Last Days? ALWAYS 175

31. What's Heaven Like? UNKNOWN 181

32. Who Will Be in Heaven? SURPRISE 187

33. The Way to Wait? ACTIVATE 193

E. GOD'S QUESTIONS TO US

34. Who Do You Think I Am? HELP ME KNOW ..199

35. Why Are You Here? I'M HIDING 203

36. What's That in Your Hand? JUST A STAFF ... 207

37. Whom Then Shall I Send? SEND ME 211

A Postscript of Encouragement........................... 215

Endnotes.. 217

PREFACE

We all have questions, many of them still unanswered. Some are just fun, brain teasers. Can you answer any of these?

What do people blind from birth see when they dream?

When you forget an especially good thought you had, where did it go?

How far east can you travel before you start traveling west?

If the early bird gets the worm, why do the good things come to those who wait?

If we humans evolved from monkeys, why are so many still running around?

At what point does it go from being partly sunny to only partly cloudy?

More seriously, some questions have far more important life consequences. We really want to know their answers and think that we desperately need to know. We search for the answers without finding them.

Frustration is common among us humans. So is pure imagination. We'll sometimes find answers to our big questions even if we have to make them up with flights of pure imagination. Will we know when that's what we've done?

River Ponderings

Huckleberry Finn is famous early American literature. Samuel Clemens (Mark Twain) captures in this novel much of the common life along and on the great Mississippi River when the nation was young. Life is viewed through the eyes of an orphan boy, Huck, and also those of his friend Jim, an old runaway slave.

They had managed to escape together, leaving behind sheer boredom for Huck and human imprisonment for Jim. Instead, they experienced a daring exploration of the wider world of freedom and adventure. They built a raft and sailed southward on their exciting way to somewhere, anywhere, just elsewhere.

Here's one brief scene. Huck and Jim would hide in the woods near shore in daylight and then maneuver their raft toward the middle of the Mississippi late in the day for more traveling in relative safety and relaxation. Out there they would settle down for the night, resting their backs on the rough deck and listening to the great silence of the vast waters.

They were escapees from the ugly conventions of civilization, being pictured as amateur philosophers and even fledging theologians of the most down-to-earth sort. Twain's capturing of their bizarre conversations is what helps make *Huckleberry Finn* great literature. What about a decent preface to Christian theology in the oddest of styles?

It once was observed by Huck and Jim that the big night sky was all speckled with stars. They gazed up at this fascinating speckling and discussed whether the stars had been made or just happened. Jim said they were made. Huck insisted on the "just happened." He thought it would have taken too long to make so many.

Jim countered that the Moon could've laid them all, why not? This massive spawning theory seemed reasonable enough to Huck once he thought more about it. He'd seen a frog lay almost as many little eggs. While this big creation question was finally being answered, a star would streak down toward earth. Jim quickly explained to the boy that it was a spoiled little light getting kicked out of the nest. That seemed to make perfect sense. Being an uneducated "nigger," thought Huck, Jim's so very wise.

So were the Indians who had their theory of the many stars. Every branch of a cottonwood tree has inside lovely black star shapes. It's believed that the Great Spirit decides when more stars are needed. He blows his breath, shakes the trees and more stars fly out, race to the sky, and as they go shift from black to shining bright. Another pretty reasonable theory.

Huck and Jim, time space travelers with their big imaginations and great theologies, would see in the darkness a huge steamboat slipping along the river in their general direction. Now and then it would send up a world of sparks out of its chimney, human fireflies joining heaven's twinkling lights. Maybe life is some kind of partnership of between heaven and hell.

The sparks would soon then rain down on the river. Huck said that looked "awful pretty." Human activity can be beautiful, especially when viewed in the dark and from a distance. Otherwise, as Huck and Jim well knew, life can be only escape from human slavery, both of them on the run themselves. The beautiful and the ugly always tend to mix somehow. Why's that?

When the sparks had shot up and settled a few times, the big boat would pass their tiny raft, go around a corner of the river, and her lights would go out of sight, leaving the little raft and its two philosophers alone again in the darkness. The water was still until the waves made by steamboat finally reached the raft long after their maker was off the scene.

There would be a little splash and a bit of rolling before the raft would regain its balance. Does God make waves? Is he long gone before we get hit and are trying to figure things out? Was he ever there or just another flight of their fancy? Would another one come along later and again threaten their very existence? So many questions, so few answers.

Once the steamboat was gone from sight and sound, it was easy to think that maybe it had never been. Then all that could be heard by little white boy and old black friend, strugglers in the dark trying to survive this world, was the renewed silence of the night. The stars were still there. What about their Maker, or was there none? If it were the Moon that spawned them all, was it alive or dead? On a cloudy night one doubts that even it exists.

Huck and Jim felt like two of those stars having been kicked out of the nest of responsible and free human society. They were on their way elsewhere, falling downward, drifting southward, hopefully to a better place and not in chains. Had there been a nest for them in the first place? If so, who had kicked them out and why? Weren't they alone responsible for running away and being free? Were they free?

Questions, so many questions about life. Truth, imagination, pure wonder, silly fancy, what's really the answer? Some questions are mere brain teasers, others soul wrenchers.

Aren't we all on that little raft looking up into the night sky, wondering, not sure if we are getting real answers? What little can be heard in the silence of our human sufferings and frantic flights to freedom? Might the next steamboat to come along in the dark fail to notice our tiny raft and crash into it? Is it safer to hide on shore when darkness falls? Is there really freedom farther south?

Is the Bible an Answer Book?

You'd think the Bible of all books would be the one volume of assured final answers. Well, it is and it isn't. It seems to leave unanswered as many questions as it answers clearly. At least it orients our questions properly, answers the biggest ones, and assures us that life can proceed without all questions answered, at least for now.

The first Christian believers faced the big life questions. Jesus posed this one. "Who do you say that I am?" The men on the road to Emmaus after the crucifixion of Jesus naturally were asking this. "How did the Romans manage to murder the man we were sure was God with us? I guess we were wrong about Jesus having been the Messiah. Mere people can't kill God!"

The Bible isn't what we often want. It's not intended to be the final answer book for all our religious curiosities. It isn't as inspired textbook for the resolution of our philosophical ponderings and ethical dilemmas. It isn't the treasure chest of trivia for our modern board games or debates with scientists or desire to win an argument with a friend. It is inspired, fully sufficient, but *only* in relation to what it intends to teach.

The Bible is full of questions from the people's dumbest to the most profound. It does present assured answers, but again only to the questions it considers most pressing for our spiritual well-being, present mission, and future destiny. The rest of the questions tend to be ignored.

Granted, human travelers like Huck and Jim, have creative imaginations and can find answers in the Bible whether they are there or not. Our task here is to ask a few of the important life questions and be as responsible as possible in offering brief answers actually found in the Bible—not in our own fanciful imaginations.

God Is Enough

Here are thirty-three of the really important faith-related questions that Christians ask and that trouble most people who think at all. Biblical answers are offered since these questions lie within the Bible's inspired teaching intention.

Why is the list of biblically answered questions not much longer? God tires of our mere curiosity and finally calls a stop to the questioning process. The Bible finishes by asking us four questions that tend to shut our mouths. Finally, we humans must realize that knowing who God is, intends, and provides should be enough for now!

When God is done with the answers, so must we be done with the questions. The last portion of the Book of Job is a supreme example of God's flurry of questions for us mere humans.[1] We are left with this ancient and humbling Irish verse:

> Be Thou my Vision, O Lord of my heart:
> Not to be else to me, *Save that Thou art*.

With this prayer comes knowledge of what our alternate preoccupations should be:

> More about Jesus would I know,
> More of his grace to others show;
> More of his saving fullness see,
> More of his love who died for me.[2]

Our many human questions fall into these critical categories:

WHO IS GOD?

WHAT CAN LIFE BE?

WHAT OUGHT THE CHURCH TO BE?

WHAT FUTURE WILL THERE BE?

1

HOW "SMART" ARE WE?

We people of recent centuries increasingly have understood ourselves as finally grown up, gaining scientific prowess and managing to take charge of the world and ourselves as never before. If there are answers to life's big questions, we'll find them and try directing them toward the human good.

A big question is this. "Just how smart have we humans become?" Especially the young now are reaching constantly for their smartphones. The newest I-Phone drips with "Apple Intelligence," "artificial" and yet increasingly very real. Didn't that apple clear back in the Garden of Eden have enough perverted intelligence to lead us away from God? What's happening with the newer fruit? Is there an "App" for everything? Is this "Enlightenment" mind-set ending? Should it be? What is it and what might be following?

An "App" for Everything?

With a mere finger swipe, most people now hope to access nearly all human knowledge, from yesterday's ancient Egypt to tomorrow's quantum physics. Artificial intelligence can think for us, create for us, find anything lost, buy anything that exists with free delivery if you buy the right plan.

The typical person now gobbles up data while messaging friends and looking at the little screens while also driving a car. From behind the wheel, one can buy something probably not needed with a swipe and a click and glance at the traffic while paying with a number on file somewhere in the "cloud." If young and late for school, it's possible to look for the "app" that's the quick way to draft the paper due in an hour, the one that should have been written by oneself last week. Life is too busy swiping and texting, buying and talking, neglecting and surfing.

As we swipe and consume and talk and buy and maybe cheat, we try not to be so distracted that we walk into walls or drive dangerously off roads. We must hurry to get somewhere, already late, possibly somewhere we don't really want to go, but at least the phone will help us find it. We steer with one hand and try managing to manipulate our whole world with the other.

We text unseen friends just to see if they know anything we don't and maybe should. Still, we aren't satisfied, only busily distracted and anxious for more of something. What's missing here? Don't we "moderns" still need thoughtful wisdom and real relationships, actual learning that doesn't come with a flood of presumed facts and words and contacts and pre-digested apps and numerous distractions?

Much remains unanswered and unfulfilled, even while billions of answers presumably are only a click away. Do we even know how to know anymore? Answers are everywhere and still the unanswered questions multiply.

Dead Philosophers, Poets, and Sinners

A journalist recently took a literary excursion in search of the best life lessons to be found in the writings of prominent but now mostly dead philosophers.[3] The published result is insightful and full of curiosities. Still, it comes down to encounters with abstract and escapist ideas of yesterday that change little us today. The deceased were quick to criticize life as they knew it. They offer a wide range of fanciful schemes for self-improvement. It's interesting reading, just not much help.

There's the supposed wisdom of the writer of *Ecclesiastes* in the Bible. He fears that life is nothing but a dreary mist that will fade away into nothing. "One generation goes its way, the next one arrives, but nothing changes—it's business as usual for our old and dying planet earth."[4] If you're going to read the Bible, don't stop here. There's real hope elsewhere in its many pages.

The famous film critic Roger Ebert recalls a famous movie scene staged in 1959 at an all-male elite boarding school.[5] A creative English teacher brings to life a few works of select dead poets, telling his students, *Carpe, carpe diem!* "Seize the day" boys, make your lives extraordinary! Sounds good, but it's only a good movie.

Revisiting deceased philosophers and poets can be inspiring, no doubt, and I recommend it. Let's get "turned on" if we can. Which dead poets or philosophers should we visit and then imitate? Will it all turn into dust shortly anyway?

For many Christians, focusing on life's continuing questions is a problem. We prefer to use many exclamation points about Christian faith visions, even periods where only commas belong. We fear question marks. Aren't we to preach the truth, be done with questions, and live by faith in known facts? Is something wrong with humility and doubt?

Is faith likely escapist and strictly personal choice? We who do believe must see that a mature person has little fear of being self-critical. Doubt is a valuable means of exposing false securities and idolatrous views. Faith and doubt are both better by being friends.

In these pages I bring off the bench thirty-three difficult and often unanswered questions related to Christian faith and put them right into the game. Maybe they will be answered while in the action. If God is really God, there's no danger of disrupting heaven with our little inquiries We must quit hiding what hurts, silencing what needs addressed most.

God isn't offended or threatened by honest questioners. We surely have the questions, and God can take it! However, sometimes the church of God can't. Reveal your true self and you might get rejected for not towing the line. "Whatever it is, when you think about it coming to light in the presence of Christian people, do you feel like you would rather die? Do you feel like throwing up or running away because you feel unsafe?"[6] Raising hard questions isn't welcome.

"Straighten out or get out!" Too strong? Yes, in some cases, but that's how particularly troubled youth often feel and thus leave. We need to hear this witness.

> If ever there was a truth that needs to be internalized, it's the amazing story of a God who spoke all things into existence, sustains creation with his breath, and loved so much that he himself came as a helpless baby to touch us at our point of need. When we weren't

understanding the immensity of God's love for creation in all its brokenness, God spoke that love in terms we could comprehend, the sound of a baby's cry on a cold night in the smell of a lowly, animal-filled stable.[7]

Have urgent life questions? Are you unsure about whether you dare approach a holy God with your unholiness? God knows all about your fallenness and at great cost already has chosen *to approach you in love*!

The Ultimate Answerer

These pages ask many of our urgent religious questions and conclude with God responding with four questions of his own. God does answer. One song expresses well the persistent feelings haunting recent generations. "Who will answer?" People are lost in unharmonized complexities, revolving in apathy, slipping to the edge of personal disaster, blurting out desperate questions about human existence. "If the soul is darkened by a fear it cannot name, *Who will answer? Who will answer?*"[8]

Christian people have the responsibility to announce that there is an answer because there is *an Answerer*. Jesus Christ *has answered*. His answer is as personal as our private longings and as extensive as the most distant reaches of unresolved reality. His magnitude equals the mysterious clashing of love and providence, good and evil, meaning and destiny. He alone has orchestrated in his own person the depths of divine truth that can resolve our question-filled human lives.

God isn't "keeping score of our screwups. He isn't the kind of God who is just out to catch us, criticize us, punish us. He wants to bring his love to our brokenness and his holiness to our humanity."[9] In other words, open up to God and bring on the questions. There's healing somewhere in the wind.

These coming short essays intend to say repeatedly, *"carpe diem!"* in a distinctly Christian context. They are brief but substantive Christian devotions, short sermons, theological musings, sinful confessions, little glances at the depths and possible heights of things. They are declarations of life in this world as it is and can be by the sheer grace of God.

All questions may not get answered to our satisfaction, but even that is acceptable. We will come to know enough to be relatively unconcerned about what, at least for now, cannot be known. Maturity doesn't demand finality.

Will you seek to hear a living word from someone other than a deceased philosopher or poet. Yes, the Jesus of long ago was killed on our behalf, and yet *he still isn't dead!* This man from Galilee has the last word in each of these little journeys into wisdom. He is the man who also is *God from heaven.*

One haunting question still echoes down the halls of time. Outside the empty tomb of Jesus, two figures speak. Using the old King James language, they ask, "Why seek ye the living among the dead?" (Lk 24:5). What follows doesn't spend much time confused in an old cemetery. It allows the Living to speak to us about life beyond.

No Final Nailing Down

The television journalist Mort Crim commends one book that encourages questions for God and doesn't think it's a betrayal of faith to have such serious questions.[10] In it Sam Collins says this.

> If the Bible is any indication, God seems more inclined to ask questions than reply to them in definitive detail. Job raised so many questions that it would have taken a committee of theologians and Oxford-educated philosophers a couple of decades just to catalog them. When God finally did to show up, the Creator did not go point by point and set Job's mind at ease. Instead, God announced, "Brace yourself like a man. I will question you and you shall answer me."

God is God! If you are crying out in repentance and love, seeking the highest good of others and wanting to be more like Christ, then God says to you, "Bring on your questions!" Check questions 34-37 here for God's questions to us.

In my lifetime I have sought to give answers to big life questions through sixty-five books and forty years of university teaching and ministerial practice. I attempt here to grasp the essence of those pages and years in a few brief essays. Give them a quick look and don't drive while you do. Distraction is dangerous.

I confess admiring the work of biblical scholar Eugene Peterson. As he labored to craft careful sentences to convey his deep beliefs, he realized that for him, and now for me, writing is a way of prayer. "He trusted God's grace and mercy so profoundly that he didn't carry the crushing burden of having to nail every question to the ground."[11] Nor do I carry such a burden or the ability to do the nailing if I did.

I hope you will dare ask the hard questions. Explore these answers to some of them, guided by the One who was dead and *no longer is*. I refer to Jesus who said, *"I am the way, truth, and life."* Either he was a deluded lunatic claiming to be God present with us or he really was and by his Spirit still is the ultimate of all things. Abandoning the lunatic option, let's see what he has to say.

God is with us, giving more than musings by dead philosophers and poets or "facts" manufactured on a distant computer by self-serving electronic geeks. Accepting this will take a little faith, of course. So does every available alternative. *Carpe Diem!*

All questions will not find full and final answers in this life. We must come to terms with this simple fact. Even so, "the fellowship of perplexity is a goodly fellowship, far superior to the fellowship of easy answers."[12] The more mature our faith grows, the less we will need all answers in advance.

2

CAN YOU LIVE WITH MYSTERY? DARE!

We believe in God who is the Mystery, that is, majestic and well beyond full human comprehension. To claim all knowledge of the divine is to be deluded. The mystery of our faith is great (1 Tim 3:16). It's also a marvelous mystery now known to radiate the love of Jesus.

The Bible says that the mystery of God is "Christ in you, the hope of glory" (Col 1:27). God is the truth, all truth, the source of all things. Jesus Christ is now revealed as the key to understanding God's very nature and thus the divine plan for our human salvation. Dare we believe this amazing claim? Can we somehow live it out so that others might come to believe?

Our world is full of mystery. Small aspects get clarified now and then. Researchers finally solved the mystery of why ancient Roman concrete lasts for thousands of years. Engineers included lime clasts in their mixture. These particles allowed concrete to heal itself when cracks formed. Water entering the cracks would dissolve the lime, which then would recrystallize and fill the gaps. Might modern buildings now last for centuries if we follow the Roman lead?

Other researchers have uncovered how monarch butterflies find Mexico during migration. Weighing less than a paperclip, they navigate thousands of miles with pinpoint accuracy. Their brains contain a sophisticated combination of sun tracking and internal clock mechanisms. This natural GPS guides to specific mountain forests they've never visited before.

Another recent development is truly amazing. There's now a way to edit human DNA with unprecedented precision. *CRISPR* technology can cut and replace specific genes, fixing genetic errors, treating complex diseases. This evolving ability to rewrite the code of life raises exciting possibilities and huge ethical questions. The more we uncover of life's many mysteries the more we are faced with our own sinful selves and questions about God, life's meaning and destiny. Science has proven quite incapable of dealing with the God question.

The Nature of "Revelation"

Any "god" we humans claim to understand fully is a mere idol fashioned in our own image. There's no alternative. Ambiguity, paradox, and mystery are inevitable for those seriously pursuing wisdom of the divine. In a Christian context. the ultimate truth is quite simple and yet very complex, now reachable although always unreachable. The message of the Gospel of John is said to be so simple that any poor soul can grasp its saving message, and yet it's so complex in its reach that no arrogant scholar has yet found the bottom of its depths.

Why the difficulty? Divine revelation as biblically understood is essentially personal, and persons have a way of transcending labels, categories, abrupt definitions, and full comprehension. God is said to be the ultimate Person eternally existing far beyond us and yet standing right next to us. What we have in the Christian faith is less a cosmic Fact delivering to us a catalog of facts about itself and more a Person, the heavenly Father actually come to be with us.

God comes intimately along the paths of our historical existence. God calls us to a faithful response to the divine Person. Religious insight and experience move toward a depth that will not yield to the captivity of simple sentences and terse definitions. Symbols, yes. Verbal prisons, no!

In traditional Christian theology, the words for this double reality of God are "transcendence" and "immanence" (high above and very near). Seeming opposites, these are equally and simultaneously true of the God made known in Jesus Christ. Paradoxically, these complimentary poles of our human experience of God compliment and do not cancel each other.

Here's the mysterious and wonderful truth now revealed in profoundly personal terms. "The more we are attracted to the one pole, the more vividly we become aware of the other. Advancing on faith's way, we find that God grows ever more intimate and more distant, well known and yet unknown. God dwells in light unapproachable and yet stands in our presence with loving confidence and addresses us as friend."[13]

The Christian gospel is truth that must not be "flattened, trivialized, and rendered inane."[14] Our human way of thinking is anxious to reduce mystery to a problem to be solved. It wrongly transforms assurance into certitude, revises quality into quantity, and turns the categories of biblical faith into supposedly manageable forms we create. We regularly fail. This frustration cries out for believers to become truth's "poets" who speak against the constant reductions of a prose world.

God Is Actor, Not Object

Christians are off track when trying to simplify the content of their faith to that which they can fully understand and control. We are to live less in our own reality more in God's. Christians often seek to grasp, codify, and protect the faith from non-believers. Their motives may be fully understandable, and in part admirable, but still self-defeating.

I suggest that we put the "fun" back into "fundamentalism," affirming the essentials of Christian faith while doing so humbly, lovingly, with both sides of our brains and all of our hearts and imaginations. We must allow for the great Mystery that brings inevitable caution to our believing. Rather than an *object* for our human analysis, God is the *Subject*, the very cause of our wonder (Ps 8:1).

There is mystery in the very timing of our faith. It's hardly appropriate to announce a period at the end of "I am saved." A period suggests finality in this life. Better to say "I am saved" followed with a comma. A child of God has experienced spiritual rebirth *and* is still growing up into the full stature of Christ. We all are disciples still in the making. On the lips of every great Christian should be humble words of honest confession, like "not that I have already attained" or "the more I know the more I realize how very little I really know."

There are multiple tenses of salvation. We *were* saved (Rom 8:24). We *are being* saved (1 Cor 15:2). We *shall be* saved (Rom

5:9). We look back to our forgiveness, rejoice in where we now stand, and look forward in faith to the time when we shall be fully like Christ. All tenses are necessary and interact. We move on in the glory and yet the mystery of an ongoing divine process.

Kamikaze is a frightening word to Americans because it recalls the fanatical suicide pilots of World War II. Now we have deadly drones directed to their targets by computers from a great distance. The word kamikaze, however, has more positive origins for the Japanese. It means *divine wind.* Apparently, in the 1200s there was a typhoon that saved Japan by blowing viciously and destroying a threatening enemy navy. In the biblical mind, there are mysterious similarities as the divine wind blows and reveals itself.

The powerful breath of God blew and creation just was (Gen 1:2). God breathed and the truth of recorded Scripture somehow was recorded and guaranteed (2 Tim 3:16-17). One day God will have heavenly trumpets blown to announce the final day. Meanwhile, the Spirit's breeze enriches humble disciples of Jesus, granting new spiritual life, special gifting, and inspired mission (Act 2:1-4).

The divine wind is not controllable or wholly explainable. In its mystery so much has, is, and yet will happen. The mystery and majesty of our faith is indeed great (1 Tim 3:16). Meanwhile,

Christian "spirituality" is personal life lived in union with Christ through a Spirit relationship with the incarnate and risen Lord. It's the Lord's death becoming our death and his resurrection ours.

Christianity is not finally a moral program or set of rules or level of ethical achievements. It's more than a philosophy of life or religious strategy for getting to heaven. Authentic Christianity is life lived *in Christ through and by the breath of the Spirit.*

Maintain the Mystery

Writing "G-d" instead of "God" is a common Jewish custom. Many believe this is an important sign of respect. It comes from an interpretation of the commandment in Deuteronomy 12:3-4 regarding the destruction of pagan altars. Some Jews avoid discarding paper or books in which God's name appears in Hebrew. Rather than being thrown out or destroyed, such documents sometimes are carefully stored or even buried in a Jewish cemetery. That's high respect in the face of divine mystery. It echoes words in the model prayer of Jesus, "Hallowed be Thy name."

While Christian life necessarily involves a "possession" by the Spirit, it isn't spooky and dangerous, being haunted in some mysterious and frightening manner. "It's being enfolded in Another, the life of God, without loss of personal control or distinctive identity. It's the means of our returning to the best of what we originally were intended to be, the first fruits of what we will yet be eternally."[15] Great indeed is the mystery and wonder of our faith.

Keep this in mind. The hiddenness of God must never be forgotten, even when we stand before God's self-disclosure in Jesus. We are to remember the depths of the divine mystery allow an appropriate awareness of the humbling awe required. The Lord knows that we are formed from mere dust. Our lives are like grass that can blossom with wildflowers and then wither into apparent nothing. Even so, the Lord's gracious love for us remains throughout eternity for those who reverence the sovereign Creator (Ps 103:13-17). The amazement of this is beyond description.

The one God truly encountered in Jesus nonetheless remains the *mysterium tremendum*, the unsearchable and hardly knowable divine mystery. God is never fully comprehended with our minds and yet amazingly can be known as available, loving, and redeeming. We ought to "fear" the Lord, not by being afraid but filled with a humbling and faithful gratitude. This knowing and reverencing remains full of unknowing. In this mix is the beginning of wisdom.

Two wise men reported their deepest life learnings. One said he had stood astonished at the immensity of things and at his own ignorance about most of them. The other applauded this wisdom but nonetheless was steadied and guided by his biblical faith. It had led him to a passionate engagement with the world as a thinking self, alert to his responsibilities while always being alive to God and humble before the mysteries of being and time.[16] This is as it should be.

****

Jesus with the Final Word

(in part a paraphrase of Colossians 1 and 4)

Paul asked the Colossians to pray for him and Timothy as they continued to preach and teach. He hoped that "God may open a door for our message so we may proclaim the mystery of Christ for which I am in chains" (Col 4:3). The term *mystery* refers to something not previously revealed. The Word of God was the mystery now having been revealed in myself to Jews and Gentiles (Col 1:25-26). It's "Christ in you, the hope of glory" (Col 1:27). I came to be intimately known by those who believe (Jn 17:3). Knowing me is to know the Father.

One Christian theology teacher shared a little testimony when he was eighty years old. He called himself a "progressive evangelical." Most important to him theologically were previous mysteries now quite clear. My Father seemed closer than ever to this loyal disciple. He sensed that my Father was "sweeter than ever." Being loyal to the kingdom that I brought near was more important to him than ever.

He concluded with this. "I'm not going to be picky or judging about anything. Playing God has never been appealing."[17] What a better church mine would be if all my disciples shared this testimony of the mystery of myself now lovingly revealed! You are to be knowing while much is not yet known. Be strengthened "according to the revelation of the mystery that was kept secret for long ages" (Rom 16:25).

3

IS GOD ONE OR THREE? YES!

"Trinity" is not a Christian numbers game. It's the best available description of the amazing God who stands, stoops, and stays. God is known by what God does. Father, Son, and Spirit are the One over us and with us and for us always. If this doctrine is puzzling, remember that the true God always is big enough to stretch our minds and even imaginations.

Don't be confused about numbers. Focus on the amazing reality of the one God who was, is, and ever will be. Judaism and Islam are clearly mono-theistic (one God). Christianity emerged from this tradition and without doubt shares this core conviction, while still standing by the importance of the Trinity.

How a Christian conceives the nature of God is basic to all that's then understood about what God does and a believer is to be and do in this world. There has been considerable controversy among Christians about the nature of God and how interacts with this world.[18] There is a persistent Trinity tradition throughout church history.

God said, "You shall be holy, for I am holy" (1 Pet 1:16). Holiness is clearly central to the divine nature and intention for believers. "Scripture thinks our greatest need is being with the God who, in Jesus Christ, has shown a remarkable determination to be with us. A vision of God, rather than merely some helpful hints for everyday living, is what Scripture seeks."[19] This vision is focused best in the person of Jesus.

Where did he originate? Was Jesus the son of Mary who became the Son of God? Or was he the eternal Son of God who became the son of Mary?

If the first question is the case, we have no good news to share. If Jesus emerged out of us humans, he can do nothing more for us than we can do for ourselves. But if Jesus came *to us* by the initiative of the eternal God, then he can do for us what only God can do.[20]

Jesus Was Before He Was

John's Gospel insists that the story of Jesus did not begin with a baby in Bethlehem. He always was the divine Word who once became the eternal expression of the creative God made flesh for our salvation. There was a pre-existence. "Before Abraham was, *I am*" (Jn 8:58).

For biblical authors, "God is not understood philosophically but *functionally*. God acts and thus is known by the nature of the actions. The ancient Hebrews thought of God primarily in terms of personality and activity, not in terms of pure being or in any static sense."[21] A modern novelist uses words that catch the vastness of the biblical vision. "There is a river that runs through time and the universe, the Spirit who is the flow of all existence, vast and beyond explanation. It's only when I yield to the river and embrace the journey that I find peace"[22] God is love, the water of life itself, known only by his loving actions.

Moses, Isaiah, Amos, Jeremiah, and the others witnessed God creating a people, saving a people, implementing justice, and offering hope for the future. The New Testament shares the news of God coming to us in Jesus. Judged by these divine actions, God is the source and measure of human salvation, justice, and hope.

A common viewpoint among many Christians today differs in significant ways from this biblical perspective. The non-biblical view goes back to Aristotle whose ultimate deity was the unmoved-mover, God understood as pure consciousness, timeless, self-sufficient, immutable, impassible. To have real relationships with people like us would mean a divine dependence, a violation of God's fixed and never vulnerable perfection. Any speaking about God by use of human terms is necessarily to reduce God to the "finite," therefore committing a subtle idolatry.

Following this line of thought, an awkward conclusion is inevitable. The Hebrew Scriptures (Old Testament), while very opposed to idolatry, appears the chief of idolators! God is understood in the Bible to be voluntarily present with us fallen humans, very relational, risking, and thus vulnerable. Suffering, supposedly never to be associated with God, is said to reveal the heart of God and announce our calling to be God's obedient and sometimes suffering children. God is love and love reaches, relates, risks, and seeks to redeem.[23] God is all of that or not the Father of the humble and crucified Jesus.

The problem is the tempting tilt toward "hyper-transcendence." The urgent need, like John Wesley once said, is to follow a personal (biblical) rather than an absolutist (philosophical) conception of God. God is not to be thought of so much as creator, judge, and king, with the emphasis on divine *control* and *unchangeability*.

Where is thought to center? It's on God as savior, lover, and friend, with the emphasis on relationality and human response-ability. Wesley viewed God "not as a unilateral power who takes no risks, but as a bilateral power who gives creatures room."[24] So does the Bible. So should we. Thinking this way helps to answer several of our urgent questions.

Granted, all descriptions of God are limited human understandings, analogies used to describe what finally is indescribable. Nonetheless, they can be meaningful metaphors that speak helpfully of the One who has become known as active among us humans in particular ways. Such descriptions are believed by biblical writers to constitute a basic and balanced understanding of God's nature and intentions.

Not Remote and Unsympathetic

A person's nature is shown in *what that person does*. Likewise, God's nature is consistent with the divine actions, especially seen in God's revelation in Jesus Christ. God is pictured by Jesus as *gracious, self-sacrificing love*. That's where the *one and three* of the *Trinity* come in. The Christian concept of Trinity "depicts God as beautiful and supremely lovable. God is not featureless, isolated and motionless, but a dynamic event of loving actions and personal relationality. What loveliness and sheer liveliness God is!"[25]

The sovereignty God is a beautiful thing because God has determined "not to unilaterally decide matters. God enlists our input, not because he needs it, but because he desires to have an authentic, dynamic relationship with us as real, empowered persons. Like a loving parent or spouse, God wants not only to influence us but is willing to be influenced by us."[26]

The church too often has presented God as "remote and unsympathetic and existing at humanity's expense." Often atheists refuse to believe because they have not been told about the real God of the Christian gospel who loves us freely, wants a joyous relationship with us, and is anxious to empower us for the best we were created to be.[27]

The dominating motivation of divine sovereignty is *love* more than the maintenance of full control of all that happens. Suffering is not inherent in God, but love is. Love opens a door to suffering. God freely wills to enter into our suffering and suffer *for* us as necessary.

It's possible and proper for us to affirm both the loving vulnerability of God and the absolute sovereignty of God. Such dual affirming is very biblical and not a diminishment of God, as some believers fear. God is so sovereign that, because of an overwhelming and compassionate love, God freely chooses to save the world *through weakness and risk* (the incarnation and the cross of Jesus).

Jesus arrived among us not as divine conqueror on a mighty white horse but as a helpless baby in a smelly animal stable. The key fact of Christian faith is that the Word became *feeble flesh*, a dramatic statement of God's relational engagement and changing unchangeability! The holy and loving God is engaging and interacting, reaching and risking, always seeking to save, even at high divine cost, all because of love.

The future reign of God now works in the world by the power of the Spirit who is introducing that reign and one day will bring it to fullness. God is present and active, a loving sovereignty who calls for real partnership with *response-able* and thus fully *responsible* disciples.

Did you catch the *one-and-three* of God? God *stands* forever, *stoops* vulnerably in holy love in Jesus, and *stays* in the Spirit to activate our redemption now and forever. The classic Trinity theological statement dates back to the 300s A.D.

"We believe in one God, the Father Almighty, Maker of heaven and earth, and in one Lord, Jesus Christ, the Son of God, essence of the Father, God of God, and in the Holy Ghost, the Lord and Giver of Life who with the Father and the Son together is worshiped and glorified."[28]

One God, always above, once with us below in the flesh of Jesus, and now as the Spirit with us to the end of age. Three—one—hallelujah! Recall the great hymn words of R. E. Hudson:

All praise to God who reigns above in majesty supreme,

Who gave his Son for all to die, that he might man redeem.

****

Jesus with the Final Word

(in part a paraphrase of John 1, 6; Matt 16; Luke 22)

"Who are you, Lord?" was Paul's anguished question to me when I confronted him on the Damascus Road (Acts 9:5). He spent the rest of his life answering this question for fellow believers. His answer, as well as John's and Peter's, is the heart of the Christian good news I brought. God has been and will be united from eternity to eternity as the Father and the Spirit, and once was joined to humanity as a real flesh-and-blood human in the Son (1 Tim 2:5), one in three, three in one, all from eternity to eternity, God!

All this was the love of the Father being expressed in me, the Son, and now ministered through my Spirit. God is one. We are a singular communion of reaching love seeking to redeem all fallen creation. This is a very big truth not easily grasped and believed. Peter once managed to (Matt 16:16) and then under pressure ran from the huge implications (Lk 22:56-60). Can you manage more? My Spirit is present to assist, and my Father always stands ready to receive. I embodied and sacrificed everything for you! My Father, the Spirit, and I truly are one, and together we love you profoundly!

4

IS GOD WEAK?
YES, IN A WAY!

Jesus was born a helpless baby, didn't manage to overthrow Rome, and was hung as a criminal. Does that mean he and his Father are "weak," even failures? Do the words "meek" and "weak" mean the same thing? Can you imagine God being totally sovereign and yet hanging on a Roman cross? You can if you are a biblical Christian!

What is God really like? How does God choose to appear and act on our human scene to reveal the divine nature and intentions? I once chose seven Bible stories that help reveal the God who really is.[29] They are dramatic, often unexpected, and on the surface even undesirable stories.

Who is God? These seven biblical tales tell us that God is very different from us and even from our usual expectations of God. The Bible reports that God is indeed *very* different! Glance at these Bible stories and you'll get the general idea. God's appearances to us humans have been surprising, mysterious, and beyond full understanding.

What Is God Like?

Here's a glimpse. God always is at least partially "unidentified" as flying like a UFO into our awareness (Ezek 1 and 37). God arranged for Mary a sperm-free pregnancy to make clear who finally is in control of yesterday, today, and tomorrow (Lev 15; Matt 1). God even acts in what we often think are ungodly ways, not flashing raw power to push persons about. Instead, God acts in voluntarily vulnerable ways, like a hapless little sheep full of self-giving love (Isa 53; Matt 5).

God desires it known as willingly to marry a prostitute, showering her with love and forgiveness despite everything she persists in doing. The church is the bride that is not always faithful to the groom, whose faithfulness is never-ending nonetheless (Hosea 1). God has a funny bone and a flare for the dramatic, willing to make a deal with a whale to help convince a wayward preacher that divine love is broader than his narrow human hate. God's creation is colorful and joyful because its Creator is like that (Ps 107; Jonah 2).

God is like a beautiful young woman whose insides shake with longing for her beloved (Song of Songs 5). God is a celestial mystery, beyond capture by our modest brains and biggest telescopes. Nonetheless, God has chosen to be made known in Jesus Christ. The divine power, love, beauty, grace, and glory outrun understandings and even imaginations. They are truths wonderful enough that we can't exaggerate their reality even with our most inflated words and enhanced images (Eph 1).

Many Christian thinkers have come to this important realization. Various negative characteristics often attributed to God are at odds with biblical revelation, even if championed by many "conservative" believers. God is *not* monarchical, repressive, unchanging, judgmental, passionless, motionless, exclusively male, or all-controlling. God is full of passion and empathy, maternally loving, daringly risking, and voluntarily suffering because of a great love that's seeking to overcome our wayward human ways.

God is always "transcendent," that is, separate from and other than us humans and our world. Even so, God also is always redemptively engaged with us on behalf of our well-being. God, while very present in the creation, is never part of it or trapped by it. God does change strategies toward the changing creation, although the divine nature and will never change. God lovingly involves the divine being in human history, having granted fallen humans freedom of choice. Therefore, God often is "risking" and voluntarily suffering as a loving means of our possible redemption.[30]

Contrasting Flowers

The manner of our understanding God's person and ways can be pictured as one of two contrasting flowers. One is abbreviated with the letters **TULIP**, **T**otal depravity, **U**nconditional election, **L**imited atonement, **I**rresistible grace, and **P**erseverance of the Saints. We humans are said to be radically fallen and unable to approach salvation with our faith. God alone chooses those to be saved, none being deserving. The chosen, a limited number, cannot resist the divine election and will be preserved eternally. All choices are God's and beyond question or alteration.

The alternative theological flower is more delicate, beautiful, and biblical. It's the **ROSE**. God is **R**elational, **O**pen, **S**uffering, and **E**verywhere active. This view of the divine is much more relational in nature, open to loving relationships freely chosen by humans, with all persons made capable of reaching in faith to God's love that first reaches toward them.

This rose-like mutuality of chosen love relationships in no way compromises divine sovereignty. Instead, it reflects more accurately the character of God and thus the nature of divine sovereignty. Salvation is made available to all persons and must be chosen and faithfully maintained. God has paid all necessary costs and now willingly risks rejection by those so loved. The resulting divine suffering is not a sign of weakness but of the amazing strength of divine love. Is God weak? Yes, in a way that reflects the nature of divine strength.

The Nature of Power

A central issue is our human understanding of *power* in relation to God. Does it focus on the ability to force others in some required direction or, more biblically speaking, the ability and will to *persuade* toward the good? Persuasion is how God typically works his loving ways. We do see in the Bible times when force became necessary, but never in God's choice about whether or not to be faithful to the chosen people.

God prefers our *empowerment* for proper choice rather than constant control and *overpowerment* that forces God's preferences. Again, this divine preference is not a sign of divine weakness. It's an expression of love, God's very nature.[31]

God comes to us humans most fully not at the head of a marching army but as a baby in a cradle with stench, disease, and death threatening on every hand. The Sovereign of the universe appears as a helpless sheep risking sacrifice, a crying infant with Herod immediately putting a price on the head of the baby Jesus.

According to the Book of Acts, Pentecost was the dramatic time in the early church when a frightened bunch of despondent disciples suddenly expanded into a bold international community of God's Spirit. They wouldn't stop talking about the resurrection of Jesus and the new kingdom launched on the human scene. The opposite side of cross "weakness" is the power of resurrection!

What had happened to explain this amazing change? Followers of Jesus had come down from their trees of doubt and fear, taken the Spirit of God into their homes like Zacchaeus did, and started being excited "fools" for Christ. They were now witnessing right in the faces of unbelievers whom they knew wouldn't tolerate such "good news" without violence.

Never mind. Fear had become unstoppable fortitude. The reason? Jesus, crucified, was alive! He indeed was God with them and for all others. Those newly Spirit-filled disciples had started saying the right word—"YES!" We can sense this positive thrust spilling everywhere on the pages of the New Testament.

"The Lord will rescue me from every evil attack and save me for his heavenly kingdom. To him be the glory forever and ever. Amen!" (2 Tim 4:18). "Amen" is the Bible's "YES!" God's coming to us in love is the divine possibility of our change. "Amen!" So be it, let's be changed! Yes, I believe, I choose to receive, and I will be made new by God's sheer grace. That's God's strength at work in us and for us as persuasion and empowerment.

Real Power Seen in Apparent Weakness

The Christian church is trying to find its way today. It should be the gathering of the "saints," the new Spirit people, the resurrection community reaching to the whole world by the sharing of God's love. Changed believers should gather for group exercises in joyful thanksgiving to God and grace-enabled growing and serving and reaching through the power of God's persuasive Spirit.

Paul told the Corinthians, and now us, that "all the promises of God in Jesus are *Yes*, and in Him *Amen*, to the glory of God *through us*" (2 Cor 1:20). The people of Jesus are to be in this world *as God is*. We can be present this way because God is with us and in us.

God's power is made perfect in our weakness. Christ, our high priest, was tempted as we and fully understands our plight (Heb 4:15-16). When we were weak, Christ died for us (Rom 5:6). When we are weak, then are we strong (2 Cor 12:9-10) because the Spirit helps us in our weakness (Rom 8:26-27).

The Lord, the everlasting God, never grows faint or weary. His strength has been shown to us in his great *Self-giving* (Isa 53). God willingly died that we might gracefully live! God lives forever and therefore so can we! The greatest of divine power has been demonstrated in the most apparent weakness. That's who God is and how God works. Love always is the key. *Amen!*

****

Jesus with the Final Word

(in part a paraphrase of Luke 1:47-55)

It's critical, my friends, that you open your minds and hearts to who my Father really is. Refuse to be captive to limited human preferences and expectations. David misread the promise of the permanence of his kingly dynasty. It would end in an earthly sense. Believers always will be tempted to misread the nature of my arriving kingdom, forcing it into their political and military categories.

You must resist such human dead-ends. Holy indeed is the One who does great things for his lowly servants, like young Mary, my earthly mother. The proud will be lost across the generations in the waywardness of their own misguided thoughts and actions. The powerful will be tumbled from their thrones. Meanwhile, I will leave my cross and escape my tomb and come to you in my enabling Spirit. I came as a tiny baby and lived and died as a "suffering servant." That was far outside human expectations, although in the center of my Father's nature and will.

I call on you to sing with Mary. She lacked answers to many obvious questions. What she did was praise the God who has all answers and was acting powerfully in her life to reverse the deadly course of your world. Here's the big lesson she learned. "You all are travelers, brothers and sisters on a continuing faith journey. You don't begin to arrive until you realize that it's been the loving and suffering God all the while having first been moving toward you."[32] My Father has come to you in me! Now go to the world through my Spirit!

5

PANIC AT PARADOX?
NO, RELAX!

Paradox is at the heart of Christian understandings of human existence. In theology, "orthodoxy" is paradoxical and yet the only straight path to true wisdom. This leave many of our questions unanswered. Even so, relax and allow whatever is unanswered to be that way for now. God's revelation isn't intended to answer in advance every question we can raise. It's more to point us in the right direction and be part of the right people.

A beloved professor wrote this in his Foreword to a book of mine. "This new book deals honestly with the nature of truth. The author is one of my prized students who wrestled for months with me on the basic question of how to combine reverence with intellectual integrity. I welcome his emphasis on the complexity of truth. I commend this writing to people of all persuasions."[33] These words point to an important fact that lies beneath all Christian theology.

That fact is like the operation of a tuning fork. A musically meaningful tone emerges when each tine is in carefully controlled tension with the other. It's like our eyes. Each eye individually views the scene before us. To get the full realism with in-depth perception, it takes their joint operation. This is the principle of paradox. "In formal logic, a contradiction is a signal of defeat, but in the evolution of real knowledge, it marks the first step in progress towards victory."[34]

The Romance of Orthodoxy

There often exists a selectivity in the portions of truth that get recognized and proclaimed at one time. Tunnel vision and halfway theologies flood the airways, the internet, and even prominent Christian pulpits. They present an open door to religious fanaticism, basic theological misunderstandings, and a weakening of the potential impact of Christians on contemporary civilization.

It's humbling to dare thinking "whole," avoiding grabbing and championing what little we understand and insisting that we have the full truth. Half is not whole. Partial truth is untruth. The demoralized "liberal" and the resurgent "conservative" elements of the Christian community today both need to acknowledge what G. K. Chesterton once called "the romance of orthodoxy."

Major Christian beliefs are a joining of at least two coordinate truths placed together delicately to form a larger whole. Each contains a vital piece of the whole. Only together do they form the essential paradox that alone is able to express the real truth, the entire truth.

Was Jesus a real man or God with us? Yes. Is the church the body of Christ or a group believing humans still spiritually immature? Yes. Did humans compose the Bible or God inspire it? Yes. Has the Messiah come or still to come? Yes.

Christians are faced with crucial paradoxes that are *inevitable* if our theology is to be *adequate*. We must avoid panic in the face of persistent paradox. These delicate ambiguities may be the only paths to true wisdom. We must learn to listen to each other again, always reaching for what's still missing in our present understanding. Who has it all figured out? No one I know.

We spoke above about the "Trinity" of the one true God. Jesus is both the "Lamb of God" and the "Lion of the tribe of Judah" (Jn 1:20, 36; Rev 5:5), a real human man from Nazareth and the only Son of God from heaven. Such paradoxes are perplexing, granted, leaving some questions unanswered. Even so, we are to relax and dare to believe *the whole* of Christian truths!

Christian doctrines must appreciate the intricate interrelatedness of the various strands of theological meaning. We believers must have patience and humility. We must recognize that truth is more than the latest discovery, the loudest voice, or the most popular creedal formula. Our humanness is anxious to stop short, find a short-cut, cheapen what is very rich.

That's the romance of orthodoxy. Our believing is to be in love with the truth, the whole truth, what's known and what's still being learned. It's to be classic and contemporary, thought out and felt deeply. Being too narrow is to have become crooked, unorthodox, closed off from what also belongs to the best believing. We need theological equilibrium, doctrinal balancing, willingness to be "caught between truths" and thus more in touch with the whole truth.

Diversity on Every Hand

We Christians now live in a time of great diversity outside and inside the church. We dare not give in to the human tendency to isolate ourselves behind closed doors of fixed and inflexible theological thinking. The crowd often is loud but wrong. Others may see a part of the truth what we don't.

We must never stop listening with loving care, for the crowd's sake and our own. It's dangerous to insist on flat yes-or-no answers to the perennial questions of life. God's thinking is well above ours. Don't be satisfied with the first thought that crosses your mind. It might be correct, but not altogether.

My wife and I were on a cruise ship. She noticed an abstract painting on deck six. Its caption read,

My brother just married a two-headed woman. "Is she pretty?" someone asked. The response was, "Yes *and* no."

Just as coins have two sides, there may be legitimate multiple perspectives on many key issues. Staying open is important. Seeing both sides is to see each more adequately.

People wish for plain and simple answers to their most important questions. What if the only adequate answers necessarily involve the complexity of paradox? What if the easy answers longed for are much less *adequate* than they are *available*. What if Christian believers offer pat answers more successful at sounding true than relating realistically to life and the whole revelation of God? In the quest for crisp and comforting answers, we modern disciples of Jesus must not settle for the shallowest of responses to the deepest of dilemmas.

Someone's fingers wander idly on a piano keyboard. The white and black keys of life jangle together in apparent meaninglessness. One day God will guide the fingers and a beautiful chord will sound from a carefully selected group of notes. It will be a harmonious echo from our discordant lives. When Christ returns for his faithful church, God who is the unity of all origins and destinies will speak the words of ultimate and final wisdom. The music of the eternities will sound, "linking all perplexed meanings into one perfect peace."[35] Answers to all remaining questions then will emerge.

We Christian "theologians" must cling to the principle of the tuning fork and embrace some basic principles of architecture. The great height of a Gothic cathedral is possible only because the central arches and flying buttresses push against each other in a carefully calculated manner. In the resulting tension, there is strength and new possibilities otherwise out of the question.

Christian orthodoxy is the theological stance that honors existing tensions and feels the push and pull of the competing elements of a given subject of the faith. This keeps them from flying apart, keeps them in proper relation to each other, and thus keeps them strong and most fully true. Remember that "heresy" isn't necessarily teaching an outright untruth. Often it is the common inability or unwillingness to be constructively caught in the middle of a complex truth.[36]

There are two unyielding facts both needing honored. When Christians seek to share their faith, there must be faithfulness to its historic foundations *and* sensitivity to what it takes to communicate effectively those foundations to contemporary hearers. To fail in the first is to have the wrong message; to fail in the second is to have the message barely heard at all. Wisdom demands that we function in the tension of such twin challenges.

The biblical book of Ecclesiastes knows that life can be fragile and fickle, frustrating even while there are a few glimpses of hope. Note that this depressing little book is placed between the psalms of David and the prophecies of Isaiah. Did the biblical editors do this deliberately? We seem to be invited to look in both directions.

We are accept a paradox of multiple perspectives, seeing hope on all sides while existing in the unresolved questions in between. One direction is sobering, the other exciting. Which is the truth? "Yes!"

Look back and hear the singing of the grateful Hebrews finally freed from long bondage (Ps 19:1-4). Then look forward and listen to Isaiah's grand announcement that the people of God are about to be set free to go home because the future suddenly is opening (Isa 60:4-5). Even when caught in the middle of apparent negatives, we are to be aware that we also are surrounded by past goodness and offers of future hope.[37] Paradox? So be it. Relax!

****

Jesus with the Final Word

(in part a paraphrase of John 2:1-11)

Let me encourage you with some personal testimony. I was thought of by most people as an ordinary young man until that day in the Temple and then that wedding day in Cana of Galilee. Soon I would be on my way to public fame that led to a brutal death on the cross, supposedly the end of me. That violent conclusion, however, was hardly the end. Things often aren't what they appear at first. Following was the shocking resurrection that would make clear to my disciples that there was nothing ordinary at all about God's work through me for your salvation.

Implementing my finished work in a conflicted world now belongs to you. Are you open to your own spiritual resurrection? Never be distracted by public acclaim. That's rarely the whole story. You always will be caught in the midst of a timing paradox. You live between my comings. You are Advent people, knowing and yet waiting and wondering. You now can come alive because of my first arrival and you will reign with me forever after my last. In between my comings, your task is to begin living the "eternal" life, the very life of my Father, and do so until I come again to take you home.

Of course, there is trouble now, but it can be survived with awareness of the glory of my resurrection vivid in your memory, my Spirit alive within you, and constant anticipation of my sure return. All that can flame your present faith into a holy fire. Don't allow unanswered questions to keep you home or slow you down. Think whole and go boldly. Keep growing and keep going!

We've begun by asking one key question about ourselves and four about God. Admitting our ignorance, what about God's mystery, Trinity, apparent weakness, and persistent paradoxes? Now come four more questions about God that really matter. They range from who really runs this world to asking, "Can You See the Star?" Jesus always is given the last word!

6

WHO RUNS THIS WORLD? BOTH!

Journalists put their personal slants on who did what and why. Who really causes world events? Where's the responsibility for terrible things like genocides? Reflect on Psalm 114. God and, by God's free and loving choice, often we humans jointly cause the events. We are fallen and yet free to choose and be responsible for our choices. Look at this world. We obviously have made many bad choices! God still is at work. God and we form the mixture of causes. We must quit blaming God when the root cause of many things lies at our own doorstep.

Our human lives in this fallen world often are forced to live in back alleys where garbage and violence and death are common. That's the hard reality. Here's the big question. Where is God in all this? Is God only on the main thoroughfares where the cathedrals are located? Is God only on the lovely seashores where the soft breezes blow? Is God with the rich and lovely or also with the broken and alone?

    I often have been able to visit both. In the cathedrals, I have seen crowds of visitors curious about the attractive architecture, but with little or no truly religious interest. On the seashores, I have seen more crowds barely clothed and bent on having a good time indulging themselves, again with no truly religious interest.

In the human wastelands of Egypt, Haiti, Zamba, Zimbabwe, and South Africa, I have seen the desperate widows and orphans wandering aimlessly about. Who's responsible for the squalor right alongside the beauty? Why the spent needles washing up on the lovely shores? When war breaks out, why doesn't God stop it—or did he start it? Where is God these days? In which or in all of these places?

Humans See Only the Surface of Things

The paths of our lives too often seem to face sharp turns and cliff edges. What's worse than those dangers is the poor light that makes it so easy to miss a turn and slip off to disaster. Many people are forced to walk down dangerous paths with no map or light to see what's ahead.

We moderns often are trudging down trails of tears like the experiences of whole nations of Native Americans following the Indian Removal Act of 1830. Says the Bible, God really was and is there, although often unseen. God has "a preference for the poor." Why then are there so many poor? Who passed the 1830 Act and why didn't God cancel it immediately?

A hurricane terrorized the East Coast of the United States and a Christian television evangelist reported that the dead were deserving of this judgment of God. On another channel, the analysis was that our human greed has caused climate change that's now spawning more violent weather. On a third channel, fun was being made of ridiculous theologians and mistaken scientists.

Who stirred these awful winds, God or us? Maybe both, maybe not. Causes are difficult to determine and rarely singular. Babylon overran Jerusalem, unbelievers crushing believers. Was it human greed and violence or the deserved judgment of God on a wayward people? "Yes!" says the Bible.

Our human preference too often is to see people as profit potential or sexual objects, not as persons of infinite value. We look at lovely wooded hillsides and flowing streams and want to start new housing developments to attract wealthy buyers. We are willing to pollute almost anything in the name of progress. Since confession is good for the soul, let me do my soul a favor.

I confess that I and we humans generally tend to see only what's on the surface of things. We remember only what we choose to remember. How easily this subtle selection process serves our selfish ends. We naturally become discouraged by the pettiness of some church people who see little but problems and allow the trivial to dominate their attention. Here's the really big question. What's real and genuinely worth perceiving and then remembering? What escapes mere self-service and lies beyond the prejudice of my private bias and personal circumstances?

What pinpoints actual reality rather than being infected by how we fallen humans are fond of falsely recalling? What has happened on the human scene that's so important, so intentional on God's part that it should shape us rather than we falsely shaping it? These questions are my most profound prayer. Who's in charge in this world? Who's at fault or to be given credit when awful or wonderful things happen?

I know at least something very basic. You, gracious and revealing God, are seeking to teach us that our human history, all those events, generations, battles and sufferings, joys and questions, have not been merely a random and empty process. What has happened ultimately has or still can have divine meaning and eternal destiny.

Why? Because You, the Creator and Ruler of nature and nations, have put a God-shaped plot into the drama of our history, making it truly *His-story*. It's Your story of a good creation, a costly involvement, and a glorious potential redemption. We humans, minor actors on stage, are obligated to do more than just sing about this being "our Father's world." We must remember and come to realize that in the end it actually is!

Let's get specific. When in the biblical story those ancient Israelites escaped their Egyptian bondage, was it just one of those numerous and annoying slave revolts? No, it wasn't even an escape. It was a deliverance. The Egyptians were baffled, the mountains trembled, and the sea had to get out of the way as You, God, were making for yourself a people.

Moses may have been up front in the march to the desert, but you were the leader and pathfinder. The Egyptians may have seen nothing divine about the whole troubling business, but that doesn't alter reality. Their surface observations may have focused on human determination and opportune events of nature. What they missed was the depth of the real happening. We humans do that all the time.

Behind the Sound and Fury

An adequate understanding of yesterday should bring one back to God. What really has happened? Where is the wisdom in all the analyzing of our "modern" days? The right perspective is difficult to discover in the pluralistic maze that prevails in the twenty-first century. It's always been you, God, hasn't it? I'm now beginning to remember and perceive properly. There is God and God's redemptive plan always active somewhere below the surface of life's wanderings and joys and tragedies. That's what I must find and follow. It's the trajectory of truth. It's the real in all the supposed reality.

A friend of mine once journeyed on the great rivers of South America, perplexed about why the boat's pilot occasionally would wander from near one shore to near the other. Why not do the sensible thing, going right down the river's center? He asked and was told why. "There's a river in the river." There's a deeper but crooked stream below the surface. Follow it wherever it goes and you will stay off the rocks and out of the mud. The middle sometimes is the most dangerous place to be![38]

Behind the sound and fury of our days, somewhere in the shadows of time and in the depths of the river there stands and moves the One who created the world and remains Lord over its peoples and events. God is not a cold, calculating manipulator of all things, and certainly not directly responsible for many of them. Nonetheless, God is the chief architect of time and eternity, the deep stream below the river of life's confusing surface. Staying off the rocks requires following the current. The surface rarely reveals what's actually below.

In the final analysis, while both always are functioning, divine *providence* is more potent than human *politics*. God is sovereign and superintends our fragile and often foolish ways. If only God's people could comprehend their divine birthright and the potential always latent in knowing God's creating and streaming ways. If only we were navigating carefully down life's river, staying with the depth wherever it happens to be.

Read again Psalm 114. Let the mountains dance again. May the rivers that still obstruct and the captors who still enslave bow before the design that is deepest in things. May I and others recognize God's hand and gladly join the trail of divine destiny (Phil 2:9-11, Rev 1:7). The Christian faith requires embracing an invisible guidance. It's taking the divine hand that's reaching for us and allowing it to lead us through uncharted waters. That hand knows the way. We often do not.

Live with this prayer. "You, my God, are still making history, not only by establishing a special people, but by ministering through this people in quiet but wonderful ways. To know and be participants in this ultimate reality is hope and life and destiny. What a realization. What a memory. What a responsibility. Help your people, God of all times, to read things well, recognizing the divine hand at work and following faithfully!

> Lead on, O King eternal,
> the day of march has come;
> henceforth in fields of conquest,
> Thy tents shall be our home.[39]

****

Jesus with the Final Word

(in part a paraphrase of Luke 21:25-36)

Friend, with the guidance of my Spirit you can make it. Help is on the way. What looks like cosmic chaos is the very arena in which my Father is delivering your redemption. God is sovereign, even in the worst of times and places. Believe that the arrival of God's kingdom is near at hand. Believe this and move on gratefully and boldly. The time is now, right in the jumble of your present lives. When the future starts happening, hold your heads high and stand firm. You are mine. Join me in reading the times accurately and being a reconciling force in shaping them.

My disciples always live in the in-between state, aware of me, waiting for me, listening to me, and coming to know me in the midst of an unpredictable world. Here's my direction. Remember my first coming, be encouraged by belief in my coming again, and choose always to live in the now, inspired by what has been and what soon surely will be.

You know the Bethlehem birth story telling of my already having come. Now long for that baby to return as the triumphant adult to reign over all, including over your own tangled life. The process already is in motion. Can you see it? Caution is in order. Don't ever allow your longing for tomorrow to paralyze your divine mission in the present. While sometimes out of sight, my Father is hard at work. In the end, the victory will be with the One who began and will conclude it all. Go in faith!

7

WHY EVIL IN THE WORLD? FREEDOM!

A group of dejected Jews put God on trial in Auschwitz. The awful evil in this Nazi death camp made all easy answers seem almost obscene. The verdict was that God was guilty of either not being, not caring, or too impotent to stop this tragedy.[40] Faith in a good and sovereign God is difficult in the midst of extreme evil. Does a good God create or at least allow evil? Why does evil exist in the first place? There are partial and satisfying answers, if not full explanations. Human freedom is the key.

The difficult question is typically not asked. "If God doesn't exist, how does one explain the presence of so much truly good in our world?" The usual difficult question often asked is, "If God is and is good and all-powerful, why is there any evil at all?" The answer is crucial although certainly not easy. Good and evil both do exist. There is no easy answer, although the Bible insists that there is one, difficult or not.

Negro spirituals have been called "songs in the night," expressions of defiant faith in the face of the degrading human slavery in early America. What responsibility do wayward humans have for this slavery? Is guilt properly placed on God? Surely the God of the Bible never wills suffering for his children. Why then was it ever allowed if God is love and all-powerful?

A former atheist explains what lies behind Christianity and why he finally came to accept it.[41] Human beings always have had the idea that they *ought* to behave in a certain way and not in others. We have an inbred sense of right and wrong and also are aware that, despite this *ought*, we frequently choose to behave in wrong ways.

This negative human choosing implies that we have the freedom to choose wrongly, turning "live" around into "evil." If God is love, then it makes sense that God would provide such freedom in creation as the necessary circumstance for enabling loving relationships between God and the creation.

Two Basic Options

There are two general explanations for why evil exists at all. They are the *materialist* and the *religious*. The first assumes that people just happen to exist. Nobody knows why because there probably is no why. The origins of everything are a series of chemical and evolutionary flukes. Oddly, we humans now just are and are capable of reasoning about the wholly irrational. Some big bang just blew us here. It's therefore absurd that some people believe in "God" and a divine creation when there is nothing like that in which to believe.

The other option, the religious, has confidence that behind all existence, moral consciousness, and human reasoning power there stands a planning and creating "Being" who is conscious, has purposes, prefers one life path for us over another, and has built that preference into human beings. God intends that there be creatures like ourselves who are deeply loved and have free wills to choose what is divinely intended. We humans are able to decide for or against the *oughts* that we sense are built into the very fabric of creation. Our freedom, divinely given, makes possible our choosing evil or true life.

Job was suffering unjustly and his friends assumed that a person who lives a good life in obedience to God will be rewarded with good fortune. Choosing evil will be punished accordingly. This faulty assumption is occasionally reported but not taught in the Bible. So why is there evil in the first place?

Common but Wrong Views

There are four common views of the presence of evil in the world of a good God. They each are slightly right and dangerously wrong. Partial answers, while partly correct, are still very wrong.

One view is that all suffering comes from God. Since God is sovereign, our lives surely are pre-planned in detail and always go as planned. The proper response? Yes and no.

Two, then all suffering must be caused by the sin of the sufferer. It's all our fault. The proper response? We do bring much harm to ourselves, but the right response to this option still is, yes and no.

Three, then all suffering must be completely random. Some people are sick and some are just criminals, no particular reason Again, the proper response? Yes and no. Buddhists claim that suffering is an unnecessary human illusion. Extinguish the desire for things and suffering will go away because we won't pain over not having what we don't want in the first place, health, money, whatever.

We long for number four and hope it exists. Job never got a direct answer from God about the cause of his suffering (Job 38 +). What he got from God was this. God is God and Job needed to become comfortable with not knowing the currently unknowable. Job finally did accept this and was satisfied. For now, admission about not knowing is better than grasping any of the common half-truths.[42] See God's questions to us under entries 33-36 below.

Let's be clear. There must be no ignoring of the injustice, violence, catastrophe, weeping, and sorrow people experience in this fallen world. What can be affirmed and celebrated is that God did not cause this or leave us to experience any of it alone. God was fully with us through the life, death, and resurrection of Jesus, and God continues to be with us now through the person and work of the Spirit of Jesus. God, by a free and loving choice, has suffered greatly on our behalf and is with us comforting, encouraging, guiding, and empowering us to persevere.[43]

Yes, God Suffers

God suffering because of our evil? Many have trouble accepting this about a truly sovereign God. That's why the cross of Jesus is foolishness to so many. Many can't accept that God is as Jesus has revealed God to be.

Jürgen Moltmann was a young Nazi soldier and Allied prisoner of war. He heard about and then saw his German homeland bombed to bits. He survived the war to pioneer the Christian tradition known as the "Theology of Hope."[44] Jürgen had found a path to hope despite the brutality of war and wrote about it in his classic *The Crucified God*. We are to view our suffering in the light of God's choice to suffer on our behalf.

The history of God's people is littered with instances of enemies invading, arrogant outsiders troubling the chosen people. The faithful sometimes themselves have sickened God with their own fallenness and evil actions. Still, because God is God, love is real and persistent. There always is hope. This arises from belief that Jesus is not merely the greatest figure in human history or the finest of moral teachers. The Christian affirms much more.[45]

Jesus, none other than God with us, willingly absorbed into the divine self our human injustices, evils, and deserved sufferings. This dramatic act of compassion, the innocent dying for the guilty, is the stunning act of love that enables our human reconciliation with God despite our own evil.

God is love and wishes genuine love relationships with all creation. Love must be chosen, and choice requires freedom among options. Evil, life lived wrongly, is always an available option. That's the Genesis story of Adam and Eve who now are us all. We sometimes choose to eat the souring fruit of the forbidden tree. The great word of Christian faith, however, is "nevertheless!" Our feelings may get crushed, our dogmas dynamited, and our questions unanswered. Still, these disruptions don't need to be the last word.

The *Devil's Dictionary* provides satirical definitions like this for "indigestion." It's "something sometimes mistaken for deep religious conviction." In ancient Greece people acting extremely on public streets were to be left alone. Why? Because it's hard to tell the insane person from the prophet of God. A Native American once said, "Plenty well, no pray. Big bellyache, heap God!" We humans have failing bodies with swirling emotions and tend to turn to God only when in a heap of trouble. God chooses to absorb our troubles out of an abundance of love.

Things to be Released

Three things must be released in light of God's overwhelming graciousness toward us sinners. They are the compulsion to be successful, the compulsion to be right, especially theologically right, and the compulsion to be powerful, to have everything understood and under control.

These seem to have been among the demons that Jesus faced in the wilderness. They are the evils intending to wreck our lives and even the life and mission of Jesus. We have the freedom of choice. So did Jesus and he chose his Father's will, even though it meant great suffering.

When our digestive systems have cleared, is God still there? Was God there all the time, suffering with us in compassion and offering hope? The Bible says, "Yes!" God can and wants to turn "evil" into "live." Ours is the holy God who issues a holy call for us to participate in a holy mission to create a holy newness in all of life.

God is the dynamic behind life's passing and often tragic scenes. God is the moving force who defies all narrow conceptual confinements. God is the living One who rises above all dead religion, the loving One who forgives all wrongs even at great cost.[46]

Why is there evil in the world? God in love has granted humans freedom of choice. For whatever range of reasons, bad choices frequently are made and consequences do come. God is love and willingly chooses to absorb our guilt on the cross of Christ, the innocent for the guilty. All about evil can't be explained right now, *but all can be forgiven and overcome*. What a mighty and truly wonderful God we serve!

****

Jesus with the Final Word

(in part a paraphrase of Luke 13:1-5)

I once was asked about some Galileans murdered by Pilate. Were they worse sinners than others because they suffered in this awful way? I said a clear "No," but warned the questioners that one day they too would perish if they didn't repent of their own sins. That's not the answer they wanted. I faced them with personal responsibility instead of satisfying their self-centered theological curiosity.

I also reflected briefly for them on the difficult issue of "natural" evil. A tower had collapsed and killed several people. Had the dead been more guilty than others and thus became the victims of this accident? My answer was repeating my first response. "No." They hadn't died because they were worse sinners. They were sinners like all people. Some things just happen without satisfying explanations available just now.

The one sure thing is the fallenness of your own lives and the available grace of a loving God, my Father. When evil leaders act unjustly or accidents happen to apparently innocent people, you quickly look for someone to blame, sometimes even my Father. There is more than enough guilt on human hands. Spend your energy addressing your own guilt. You would be wise to recall what my Apostle Paul once said. God will comfort you, and thus you will be able to comfort others faced with any affliction (2 Cor 1:4-5).

8

HOW ABOUT A GOOD IDOL? TYPICAL!

When unsure if God really is in charge of world events, or even exists at all, the easy decision is to make our own "gods." Frustrated humans always have done this, sometimes even in the church! Sorry, Moses, but the gold looked so good that your brother Aaron couldn't help himself. So many can't!

A good idol can look exceptionally good when nothing better is known. Many are not statues standing on pedestals with birds perched and relieving themselves. What about looking really beautiful or having a car the envy of all or a huge bank account? People often worship things that are silly, helpless, and momentary.

I spent much of my professional life in seminary either studying as a graduate student, teaching as a trained scholar, or in administration trying to make things work smoothly for other students and teachers. I heard early that "the call to preach is the call to prepare." The gospel of Jesus Christ is precious and should be handled with all the skill we can muster and all the inspiration the Spirit will provide.

Having said that, I also believe strongly that the case of Aaron should keep us scholar-teacher-ministers quite humble. We can pass every seminary class and still go down the wrong road. What we do in school is critical but apparently not everything that's needed. We are minds and hearts and wills. Things can change quickly as it once did for Aaron long ago after the glorious Exodus from Egypt.

Bring All Your Jewelry

Moses was younger than his brother Aaron but still the one who always seemed to get the long end of every stick. Aaron had to take a backseat and didn't take second place all that well. Moses went off to Egypt on an amazing divine career and then back out of Egypt leading a new people of God. Meanwhile, brother Aaron quietly went into the traditional Jewish ministry and generally faded from public prominence. He did well as a priest, but standard religious ritual was only a narrow slice of public life, hardly the prestige of his younger brother.

Aaron's destiny seemed more a holding of the fort than an exciting crossing over the frontiers of God's tomorrow like little brother Moses. Something in Aaron's heart was unfulfilled, even seething at his brother's privileged positions and big recognitions. One day the seething would flash into a roaring and ugly flame.

Moses was eighty when things came to a head for him. There had been a burning bush, a dramatic divine presence, and the commission to be the bringer of an entire new future for the people of God. What an amazing call! In Aaron's eyes, however, it was just another unfair smack in the ribs. Like the parable of Jesus about the prodigal son, the party was thrown for the wrong brother. Accolades went to the one who went out kicking up his heels when the loyal son was willing to stay home and do his assigned religious thing. While having the best of seminary training and quality ministerial experience, Aaron lacked something of importance deep in his soul.

Now Moses was up on Mt. Sinai, presumably doing some heavy business with God on behalf of the people's future. Meanwhile, seeing an opening below, Aaron decided that his time had come. He went into action, tired of playing second fiddle. It's so easy to serve in God's name although out of one's own hurts and needs. It's also easy to believe that a "god" in the hand is worth more than one supposedly up on the mountain out of sight and sharing secrets with big brother.

Whatever the motivation, Aaron held a religious service never taught in any seminary I know. He staged a big collecting of all the gold the people had and directed craftsmen to fashion a divine Golden Calf. When finished, he called for music to launch a frenzied dance around this precious "divine" thing. Mindlessly, the people now were worshipping a "god" that had just been manufactured out of their private possessions!

Desperation? Stupidity? Personal pay-back? Was it classic faith collapsing before a secular culture not tolerated any longer? Maybe, probably, no matter. Without doubt it was another symbol of us humans at our worst. We grab what we can and go for what we see. We fool ourselves into thinking that what shines brightest in our eyes is better than the God who supposedly resides in the clouds beyond our sight.

We idolatrous humans take what we can get and call it good enough. Aaron had decided that Moses and God could keep doing their thing, if there actually was anything being done up on the mountain. It could have been only so much thunder with Moses already dead.

Humans at Their Worst

There now are new Aarons living not far from you. Golden Calves are easily manufactured or just thought up. We must choose carefully the music to which we dance, the images to which we bow, and the religious leaders to whom we listen.[47] Are you hearing music that disturbs you? Can you focus on the mountain's "thunder" that just could be God's voice? The people of God just freed from Egyptian bondage couldn't, and later they would struggle when forced to watch their Babylonian captors parading in front of them their silly gods.

The number seven was special in Hebrew culture. In the Bible there are stories about the seven ways people are truly pitiful, seven ways God is known to be so very different, seven ways that the synagogue and church have gone badly wrong, and seven ways serious believers might go right in the future. These groupings of seven form a biblical storybook that's off the beaten track and brings us face-to-face with today's toughest issues and best solutions.[48] Here's a glance at just one.

The prophet Isaiah reports having been forced to watch a ridiculous parade in Babylon that had its humorous mishaps suffered by the local gods. "They do not know, nor do they comprehend; for their eyes are shut so that they cannot see and their minds cannot understand. Bel bows down, Nebo stoops, their idols are on beasts and cattle; these things you carry are loaded as burdens on weary animals. They stoop, they bow down together; they cannot save the burden, but themselves go into captivity. 'Listen to me (says God), O house of Jacob who has been borne by me from your birth. I have made, and I will bear; I will carry and will save'" (Isa 44:18; 46:1-4).

What? It's a parade of national idols, some tied on large animals struggling down the street with crowds cheering and the captive Jews staring blankly. One idol suddenly leans dangerously to the side and can't be saved! It crashes into the ditch, lost in its own embarrassment. The Jews couldn't help but remember. God once had freed them, carried them, saved them, but they were faithless. Now they were paying the price, humiliated in the midst of helpless "gods" who had to be carried themselves and pulled out of ditches. Who is able to save who? People get this all wrong!

Making and loving idols is an ancient and perverted human fixation. As another Bible-related story goes, Abraham, father of the Jewish faith tradition, was still a kid when his father ran a successful idol shop. A business trip took Terah away and the boy was trusted to run the place and sell all he could. An old man came in anxious to buy. Unfortunately, Abe posed this question. "Why would a mature person like yourself want to buy and worship an idol that was made only last week by my father, an idol with no brain?" The man was stunned and walked out with pockets still full of cash.

The boy had good theology but terrible salesmanship. A woman came in next with a basket of bread to offer to the idols, a humble sacrifice to the great ones. She would pretend to fill their little bellies before buying her pick. Abe, knowing the digestion-challenged things couldn't actually eat, let slip some sarcastic comment. She also left without a purchase. Then the boy made a decision, a rash act of teenage terrorism.

He smashed all the idols in the store with a hammer, except the biggest one who got the hammer jammed into its helpless hand. Dead gods were all over the place and there was not a penny of profit in the shop. Dad soon came home.

"What happened, boy?!" The answer was a calculated lie from a guilty god-killer. "A woman came in, Dad, with food for your expensive creations. They were rude to her, all wanting to eat first. The big one took charge, grabbed a hammer and smashed them all so that he could have everything for himself. There he stands, still holding the deadly hammer. To get even for this awful crime, Dad, you may want to smash that big one yourself."

Terah was speechless, ruined, and angry. "Come on, Abe, that makes no sense. My idols don't have minds that can think, arms that can smash things, and mouths that can chew. Surely you're making all this up!"

"You got me, Dad. Maybe the big guy didn't do it, but why do people pay good money for things that you admit are so stupid and helpless? Why do they worship what can be smashed with one quick blow?" Terah had no answer, only a bankrupt business plan and a guilty teenager who preferred the God who could take care of himself and his people.

What answer have we as we make, feed, parade, and sell our own idols?[49] Maybe they can't eat, but they do addict and consume us. Can we allow God alone to be God? When any nation wants to be "great," even at the expense of others, patriotism has become a poison. Idolatry is an awkward exchange. "My people have exchanged their glorious God for worthless idols" (Jer 2:11). In the process, God's people have committed two sins. "They have forsaken me, the spring of living water, and they have dug their own cisterns, broken ones that cannot hold water" (Jer 2:13).

****

Jesus with the Final Word

(paraphrase of Matthew 6 and 23)

My friends, idols aren't only statues before which people kneel, with pigeons perched on top for purposes quite other than worship. They are whatever you love and serve, often selfishly and always uselessly. I warn you about the dangers of loving money and possessions more than loving my Father. Face it. "No one can serve two masters. Either you will hate the one and love the other or you will be devoted to the one and despise the other" (Matt 6:24).

Bulging bank accounts mean nothing when you breath your last. I had several unpleasant conflicts with the religious leaders of my day. They loved their prestigious titles and the esteem they received from others. Beware of teachers or preachers or internet advertisers who display all sorts of capital letters after their names every time they write anything or appear uninvited in your inbox (Matt 23:5-12).

Be careful about being like the Pharisees I knew who broadened their phylacteries and lengthened their tassels to make themselves look more important. Fashion parades are hardly what honors or pleases my Father. Just see to it that your name is written in the big Book of Life. Names without titles are being listed there.

9

CAN YOU SEE THE STAR? IT'S ESSENTIAL!

God shines brightly but only some can see. We humans learn identity through observed actions. A noun comes to life only through verbs recognized and followed. We can't reach the divine merely with our reasoning, figuring out life's biggest questions like a simple math problem. God's too big a Noun for our brains until God acts on our human scene, offering characteristic Verbs that point properly to his true identity and purposes. *God is what God does.*

And what has God done? God once shined as the Star of the ages. It was a quiet night in Bethlehem. A few saw. Most didn't. A baby cried. Some came from afar. God smiled. Can you see it? Will you follow the star and find the Christ? If you do, you will find God with us bringing hope and a future.

The world is a chaos of sight and sound. Advertisers aggressively compete for attention. Many of us now wear headphones to shield ourselves from all the noise, only to fill our ears with our own chosen sound so that we still are not able to hear the quiet voice of God. Some of us are prone to hear voices when there are none. Some are seeing electronic "realities" that are known not to be real.

Sorting out the sights and sounds and penetrating the silence for hints of God's gentle music are the great human challenges of our time. My wife and I have been to two venues of *Sight and Sound* in Missouri and Pennsylvania. One production was "Noah." You would think you were actually on the ark with all the animals!

God Wants to be Seen

Selective deafness is a modern malady. So often the Bible calls on us to hear the voice of God. Will we? Are we able? The Bible's grand announcement is that there is divine music in the air! Can you hear it? Can you distinguish the divine voice from the massive noise of the dizzying world?

Of all people, only a few heard the heavenly music and saw the star above Bethlehem. Some saw but judged wrongly, thinking it was some exotic novelty, maybe something deceptive, even dangerous. But a few shepherds and international travelers were more hopeful in their expectation. Some headed home to check it out and others asked for directions from King Herod. He decided not to take a chance in case these strange foreigners were right. If all the fuss meant that a baby king had been born nearby, it must be eliminated quickly!

What was that star that leads to Jesus? A super-nova explosion, a conjunction of planets, a

comet, a mere illusion? Maybe, likely not. No matter. It may have been any star in the night sky that had gained a depth of meaning because some care enough to see the meaning available in all stars. They sense divine love that moves the stars, changes worlds, and comes to redeem. The New Testament isn't endorsing astrology, of course. It's affirming those who seriously search for God and are enabled by God to really see.

Once the star of God is seen and understood, we will know at least this much. God *wants to be found* and lays markers to point the way for persistent searchers. The question is less, "what was that star that guided the Magi to Bethlehem?" It's more, "how anxious are we to find the God who is actively looking for us?" Then, once seen, "how willing are we to leave our comfort zones and become participants in the divine shining?" Those looking and willing are more likely to see.

The Christmas story is about the light having come. Jesus soon grew and announced dramatically, "I am the light of the world!" (Jn 8:12). When seeing things through his lens, we see correctly. Walk the ways he illumines and soon we will find home. The Greek "epiphany" means "shining forth." It's an excited sharing of God's glory now come in the birth of Jesus, seen and understood by only the faithful few.

The Mystery Revealed

Paul says that knowing God is a search for mystery, a marvelous mystery that *wants to be found*! (Eph 3:1-12). "Mystery" shows and novels keep us guessing until the end about who did the awful thing and how. With God, the mystery of the ages had been dropping clues and finally in the coming of Jesus we have been found by and can glimpse directly the great mystery we are seeking.

Our moment of glory comes when we humans realize that we are the hunted, the ones sought by God to bring fullness of life. We then see that the awful thing done, the cross of Jesus, and are helped to realize that it was done for us, not by us or against us but *for us*. Here's the mystery in a nutshell, the plot of the ages, the truth revealed by the divine star.

The community of Jesus, guided by his Spirit (Eph 3:5) and enabled by the Father's grace (Eph 3:2, 7-8), has received the mystery of God's being and will (Eph 1:9). The church becomes God's people by receiving with gladness this mystery of God with us in Jesus. It remains its intended self only as it embodies and communicates to the whole world the amazement of this marvelous mystery. The light must be reflected and never hidden.

To shine is why we are the church. "You are a chosen nation, a royal priesthood, a holy nation, God's own people *in order that* you may proclaim the excellence of Him who called you out of darkness into this marvelous light" (1 Pet 2:9). Shining as the star, however, will take more than merely spotting it in the sky.

An old Cherokee gave his grandson this wisdom about life. "A fight is going on inside us. It's between two wolves, one very good and one very evil." The boy wondered aloud, "Which one will win?" The answer, "The one you feed." Christian holiness is not about *us* as much as about Jesus Christ *in us*. The goal is learning to reflect his image. This requires regular and disciplined feeding, spiritual battery power.

Christian people today are not so much in need of new strategies for bringing people to Christ as themselves truly seeking the face of

God. It's God's radiant glory that will attract other people, never to us but always to him. Holiness is being full of the Master, the Holy One. Jesus is the Master, the star who is to become visible and radiant in and through us.[50]

Not Too Fast!

Genesis reports that creation wasn't much until the breath of God swept over the waters. It was without form and densely dark but then took shape and blazed with light and life. We all need such formation and light, a re-creation of life that comes from God breathing graciously on us and then shining through us. It's time to exhale the foul air of our dark yesterdays and breathe in the wind of God's new creation.[51] That means being holy as God is holy, Gods breath filling our life lungs.

The mission life of the church of Jesus began with a "not too fast!" instruction of Jesus. His disciples were to delay their urgent world mission and first wait (Lk 24:49). The best going is not leaving too soon. To be effective in life and mission, Christian believers are first to breathe in and taste the living Spirit of God. Only then is there readiness to share the good news of God through the Spirit with all people.

Recall this prayer: "O God, I need a Master. Chain me back into freedom. Darken me back into light. Stab me back into wholeness. Quiet me back into singing. Erase me back into fullness."[52] In other words, make me shine as the light of Jesus through reflections of his Spirit now breathed in me.

To shine, we first must see. To see, we must look in the right place. Bethlehem was a little nowhere place in contrast to the everything of Jerusalem just a few miles away. Do we really wish to come to know God? Apparently, we must start at the bottom where we're currently stuck, in the surprising nowhere place where God chooses for Jesus to be born. God's star manages to shine in all the back alleys of the world. The darker the background, the brighter the foreground.

Says Paul, "We look not at what can be seen, but at what cannot be seen, for what can be seen is temporary, but what cannot be seen is eternal" (2 Cor 4:18). The good news of Christian faith is that what cannot be seen without aided eyes now is ready and anxious to be seen shining in Jesus Christ.

Christian believers can glimpse by faith what for now is largely out of sight. It's God quietly at work. In Jesus, time and eternity were fused and chose to shine brightly. Jesus belonged perfectly to both worlds, the visible and invisible. To realize this and live in this light is to approach holiness that's akin to God. Dare we still think in this dramatic and hopeful way?[53] The opportunity still shines in the night sky of this fallen world.

****

Jesus with the Final Word

(in part a paraphrase of Matthew 2:1-12, 3:13-17)

Those royally dressed men from far away gathered around my dirty little crib and kindly delivered expensive gifts. Were they fully understanding who I was and what my Father was doing in my coming? Not really, but that's not the point. Who does fully understand when approaching God, or rather when God chooses to approach them? The point is that these so-called "Magi" found their way to me and were honoring me with what they knew and had to give. You, my dear disciples, are still understanding only in part. Stay close to my teaching Spirit and give all you have.

The story of the Magi told by Matthew immediately highlights something very important in this fallen world. My coming was first seen by "outsiders." My Father, sovereign over all, is the divine lover of all people. Everyone is looking for the higher truth, the God above the gods. It's your privilege to go and tell them what their own Magi found long ago. The guiding star still shines. You now know his name. The water of my baptism signaled the blowing of divine wind, the power to reshape creation itself, the shining of a new reality for all who will. Keep "all" in mind. There will be the temptation to focus only on those like yourselves and practice "insider evangelism." Those shepherds and magi were "outsiders" who saw and knew first. Never forget the foreigner, widow, and orphan.

My Father's kingdom is shaped in the "the image of the invisible God" (Col 1:15). The arriving divine Spirit is the same Spirit who enables persons like you to be baptized into the community of the Spirit. True Christian baptism is much more than an act of becoming wet in church. It's a deliberate sign of having really seen the Christmas star which leads to voluntarily and gratefully being immersed into the life and mission of my arriving Spirit.

10

WANT TO BE "RADICAL"? BE CAREFUL!

Is a faithful follower of Jesus an extremist, a counter-cultural person acting against rigid religious establishments? Is it someone who just doesn't fit in? Yes, at least in the world's eyes. A Christian "radical" is a believer who chooses to do what's necessary to readjust present church realities to God's way of being and doing. Such a radical revision involves looking back to the faith's foundations and daring to be fully faithful to them regardless of consequences.

If this description of a religious "radical" is you, do be careful. Be sure your agenda is God's and not merely your personal preference. Also, be aware that Jesus didn't fit in and wound up rejected by his own people. There are costs to being the real people of God. Do whatever God directs, of course, just be sure that it's God's Spirit and not your own motivating the actions. Anticipate that there will be uncomfortable consequences. Church people rarely appreciate aggressive counters to their most sacred assumptions.

Being a "Holy Nation"

Being "Christian" is a particular way of being reconciled to God and then living in the world as a faithful representative of that reconciliation. It's a distinctive way that must be walked carefully or it will go wrong and undercut itself. The Christian community is intended to be counter-cultural, definitely in this world but clearly not *of it*. It exists in contrast to everything foreign to the arriving reign of God as introduced by Jesus and now being implemented by his Spirit.

Being Christian is a wonderful and also a difficult thing. The church is to be God's "holy nation" (1 Pet 2:9). Members are to be citizens of God's new realm and rule (Phil 3:20). While existing in all countries of the world, the church everywhere is to be a body of "resident aliens." Being on God's mission requires first being true citizens of heaven. Whatever national passport is being carried, ultimate identity is on a sacred document issued from above. Patriotism is fine f kept within bounds. Pride of place must not overwhelm being a citizen of God's kingdom first and foremost.

Entrance into the Christian life is itself to be radical. It requires deep repentance of the old life and a "conversion," a significant turning around to face God, coming to know God, and beginning to walk in a new direction, the divine way. It's the way of Jesus, radical indeed since it requires visiting his cross and becoming willing to carry own's one. Turning around brings with it this critical "church" decision. What body of Christians should be joined?

Some groups of Christian people are sharply "denominated," that is, formally established around a given tradition or personality of the faith and vigorously loyal to that distinctive establishment. Other Christian groups are tied closely to a particular nation of the world. Some are "high" church and others "low," rich in tradition and long-standing structures or much more flexible and informal.

A few church bodies are suspicious of all church institutionalism. They choose instead to focus on the requirements for membership being limited to clear evidence of fresh life in God's dynamic Spirit. This evidence is defined in various ways. There is only one church but many "churches." Which is the one for me? Does God even care?

Where I Started

My early church environment was hybrid in nature, two groups each decidedly Christian, one considerably more "radical" than the other when it comes to religious institutionalism. One is especially resistant to formal creeds and all structures hinting of "man rule" in church life. The other began in opposition to slavery in the United States, renting church pews that discriminate against poor believers, and restricting the Holy Spirit's freedom in church worship. Otherwise, it is somewhat "high" church.

One is very appreciative of the Methodist tradition in general. The other is reacting strongly to the numerous and rigid organizational structures of contemporary Methodism or any other such tradition. It's determined to be the church *of God*. Both are radical in their deep commitments to the Bible's determining Christian truth and practice.

John Wesley tried to be a loyal Anglican while vigorously introducing fresh forms of church life that turned out later to be Methodism. Fresh life outside old structures easily morphs over time into new structures. Such is the church in the world.

Therefore, I was formed as a young Christian "radical" by two comparable and somewhat contrasting church traditions, both strongly "holiness" oriented.[54] Initially attending a "free church" seminary (Church of God, Anderson) and studying nearby under a prominent Quaker philosopher (David Elton Trueblood), I learned that church history is filled with reforming (often low church) movements.

Apparently, church life tends to fossilize over time and needs occasional shafts of new light and fresh air. Even a "radical" (Anabaptist) faith tradition may require its own radicalization on occasion. I remember my home congregation holding two "revivals" each year. I wondered why members kept dying each six months and needing the urgent help of an outside evangelist for religious resuscitation.

Christian "radicals" live on the margins of the secular culture and in some ways even at the edges of the established cultures of the church. They teach that the Master resists church institutionalization at the expense of Spirit life. Jesus launched the church as a Jew ministering on the margins of Judaism's establish life. Radicals in church history have gone under many names—anabaptist, holiness, pentecostal, free church, monasticism, Quaker, Mennonite, and more recently the Believers' Church.

All of these have broken from some church establishment judged compromised. They have sought to introduce new spiritual life into the people of God. With all their diversity, there have been common themes of how Christian faith is to be viewed theologically and lived out in disciplined communities. I have reviewed these themes elsewhere in detail.[55]

Pilgrims and Politics

The Bible tends to be read by radicals from the perspective of a persecuted, suffering people. Almost all New Testament literature was preserved initially by a persecuted, suffering church that kept only those writings judged worth dying for. It's no wonder that believers in the radical Jesus tradition have found Scripture so powerful and sustaining. They have joined the early church in reading God's revelation through the eyes of pain.[56]

There is something central to the concerns of true Christian radicals. The church needs to affirm individual dignity, but without elevating individualism. It must encourage community among the faithful without authorizing the lordship of any persons, structures, or traditions in the church community.

Highlighted always is the authority of *being* truly Christian and being truly *gifted* by the Spirit for Christian life. The church must be committed to the reign of God, not to any power arrangements and perverted values of this world, including ones that may be found inside church establishments that are humanly devised.

The God-intended metaphor for the Christian life is *pilgrim*, even a martyr in extreme circumstances. The church's "political" task is the formation of a people "who see clearly the cost of discipleship and are willing to pay the price. The church exists as an adventurous colony in a society of unbelief."[57] This involves taking seriously Christ's call to an exclusive and costly attachment to him and his Father (Matt 7:24; 8:18–22; 10:34–39).

Paul's calls believers not to be conformed to the values and power arrangements of this evil age (Rom 12:2). To be authentically Christian, basic life orientations must grow out of being transformed by the Spirit of God into the image of Jesus Christ. Such must be the case regardless of any church arrangement that functions in place of the ministry, guidance, and gifting of God's Spirit. Are you prepared to be such a Christian "radical"? Be careful. It's not an easy way.

A biblically based integration of Christian revivalism and socially reforming activism was in clear evidence among Christian radicals in the nineteenth century. More recent generations of "evangelicals" have chosen instead to put heavy focus on doctrinal purity in contrast to "progressive" proposals for social justice. Others remain passionate about the necessary interface of God and the crying needs of this world.

These represent two contrasting models of Christian radicalism. They are not intended to be mutually exclusive. One can argue that "evangelicalism" has been most effective when identified clearly with the experiences of the poor and disenfranchised.[58] Christians have the challenge of determining how God's new creation should compel believers to be change agents in society at large, joining spiritual fervency with commitment to participating in God's world-changing mission.

The church is the "radical" community of the Spirit. All members are to be liberated to the life that God intends (2 Cor 3:17-18). The Spirit community is an alternative to the communities and ways of the world, a new-creation community that shares and celebrates Christ's intention and commands. Whatever cost is required to establish and maintain this community, it must be paid. True disciples of Jesus have inherited a momentous mission. They are to be nothing less than "a light for the nations" (Isa 49:6) sent as "lambs in the midst of wolves" (Lk 10:3). Like the Jewish prophets of old, at times they will collide with resisting kings and priests alike.[59]

****

Jesus with the Final Word

(in part a paraphrase of Luke 12:49-56)

Some of my words sound harsh, I know. "I came to bring fire to the earth!" I may be the Prince of Peace, but I also came to bring judgment and, as necessary, even sow unavoidable division. Grace and judgment are not mutually exclusive. Your role as my disciples is to assist people to understand all of this. My Father finally will do the needed judging. You are to concentrate on being instruments of holy cleansing and reconciling love inside and outside the believing community.

This is possible only after being cleansed and gifted yourselves by my Spirit. Only the holy ones can do the most difficult aspects of my holy work. Hear well my harsh words. Why can you understand weather conditions by checking the wind and sky and yet cannot or will not realize what's going on in the world around you? Dare to judge yourselves. The fire I bring means that my church must not be just another group of standardly "religious" people. I intend real change in my disciples and in all their social interactions.

If you see that as uncomfortably radical, you aren't ready to be my disciple. I upset many things and paid a high price. Comfort isn't always possible. Are you ready for that? If you are going to be my unflinching and deeply loving followers, you will meet resistance and must absorb it as I did, not as the rest of the world does. Live and love regardless!

11

LIVING A HOLY "YES"? ABSOLUTELY!

Are we Christian believers a "mess" or a "message"? If filled with the fruit of the Spirit of God, we will be a healing "YES" message to our best selves, others in need, and even to the Earth that now cries out in pain from our greedy living. Christianity isn't a constant negative, "I can't, I shouldn't, I won't." It's the ultimate positives, "God is, I can, the Spirit will, and the future is open and full of hope. YES!"

Holiness is a vigorous affirmative, not a life-strangling negative. Let's be done with the stereotype of religion being a damper on all that's fun. Jesus was a personality welcome at parties, loved by children, and engaging to crowds. His harshness was saved for those who were making a mockery of the Temple and allowing technical rules to overrun the life of love.

New Testament writers often conclude prayers with "Amen." This word meant more than "I'm done and we finally can begin eating." It carries a burst of rich theological and ethical meaning, like when Paul ended his second letter to Timothy this way. "The Lord will rescue me from every evil attack and save me for his heavenly kingdom. To him be the glory forever and ever. Amen!" (4:18). The reader can sense in that last word a "Wonderful!" and grateful "YES!" God did and now I am and can!

"Yes" or Only "Maybe"?

The "Amen" at the end of the Lord's Prayer is intended as the keynote for our beginning of the holy Christian life. Having laid our lives before God throughout the prayer, we are instructed by Jesus to end with the great word of faith and commitment. God has done all for us and now we are privileged to lead new lives in Christ by God's power. "Amen!" It's the divine "YES!" Because of the coming of Jesus and the power of his Spirit, we now can and should be and do just that.

The captivity was over for ancient Israel. It seemed like a dream too good to be true. "When God returned Zion's exiles, we laughed, we sang, we couldn't believe our good fortune. God was wonderful to us and we are one happy people" (Ps 126:1-3). God had spoken the divine "Yes" to his people's future. Now they were to become a large "Yes!" to the world on God's behalf. Since God has, we can and will be liberated. We have reason to rejoice and an assignment to rebuild.

Paul told the Corinthians that "all the promises of God in Jesus are *Yes,* and in him they are *Amen* to the glory of God through us (2 Cor 1:20). What is in Jesus now is to be flowing through us to others by the cleansing and empowering of the Spirit. God's angel told the compromising Laodicean church that Jesus is the *Amen* in sad contrast to themselves. The commitments of that congregation had become mixed, drifting from a clear *Yes* to a mushy *Maybe.* They had become caught in the morass of themselves rather than in the message of Jesus.

Christian holiness dares to look away from all the maybes and throw itself into the cleansing pool of God's redeeming grace where the fullness of the *Yes!* resides. We are to place our faith in the One who sits above time and is in charge of eternity. We now belong to God and are to be reflecting the divine character in this world, enjoying divine fellowship and resources that come from beyond this world.

A Mess or Message?

I gladly witness to having found the precious place where the enabling and healing waters of Jesus Christ run quiet and deep and always. I want to be immersed more deeply into these waters, turning "yes" into "YES!" My adequacy for being a child of God impacting this world lies in the constant availability of these grace-full waters of Christ's prevailing presence. A humble woman in India once saw these redemptive waters bubbling out of the holiness evangelist E. Stanley Jones.

"With the Holy Spirit, Brother Stanley is not a *mess* but a *message*."[60] As a Christian missionary to India, Jones at first had taken with him a Christian theology neatly tied up with a blue ribbon and quite defensive of any questioning by the strange theologies he encountered on this mission field.

Eventually, however, Jones had come to place the securities and defensiveness of his faith on the altar and become free to explore and appropriate any good or truth found anywhere. He reports that this gracious openness released him to *love* rather than *pity* India. In 1938t this cross-cultural love earned Jones *TIME* magazine's designation as "the world's greatest missionary evangelist."

Today's world hardly needs more NO's thrown at it, defensive evangelists who criticize harshly the foolishness and failures of others. Rather, it needs to hear and see a humble and open *YES!* like it's never heard or seen before. This big positive comes only from a hearty acceptance of the call of God to the holiness of his people that causes a reaching outward in love. Just like in the coming of Jesus, God didn't send the Son merely to point an accusing finger but to help the world come right again (Jn 3:16-17).

The heart-cry of Jesus to his first disciples has not changed with the passing of time. Praying the proposed model prayer of the Master with all our hearts and then leading lives of self-surrender before a holy God are sure evidence of the good news in action. It may be the only news the world will be willing to hear. Can the church be a message and not a mess?

This self-surrender yields redeemed people delivered from evil and ushered into the community of faith that we call the church. According to Jesus, the church should be a unified body of believers coming together in Christ on behalf of a lost world that is really loved. The Lord's Prayer is something of a "holiness manifesto" delivered by Jesus to his disciples. It's a call to center on what's most important, to be what's most positive, to go as a message of saving joy.

The goal of Christian faith involves nothing less that the "fruit of the Spirit." This is the cluster of divine life traits and spiritual abilities that make possible effective church life and mission. Some branches of this lush fruit are identified in Galatians chapter five. When our character and behavior can be traced back to the presence and functioning of this fruit of Christ's Spirit, we then will have arrived by divine grace at what may be called "sanctification" or "perfect love." This is not a pious reduction of joy, a limitation of allowable fun, a strangling of life by restrictive religion. It's a release into the largest available positives of life as it should and can be lived.

Central Are Grace and Love

Lines from a hymn of Charles Wesley express the heart-cry of every Christian believer who has listened carefully to Jesus and now is praying and living in his very positive and joyous way. It comes from the decision to say YES! to God and to do all that God expects and makes possible.[61]

> Love divine, all loves excelling, Joy of heaven to earth come down,
>
> Fix in us Thy humble dwelling, All thy faithful mercies crown.

A modern paraphrase of the Lord's Prayer ends helpfully with this awareness of God: "You are in charge! You can do anything you want! You are ablaze in beauty! Yes! Yes! Yes!"[62]

I echo the following words of E. Stanley Jones, so hoping to *be* the message of the Lord's Prayer. "So I live in a state of 'Yes-ness.' Yes! to the Lord Jesus; Yes! to life and its responsibilities; Yes! to approaching death; Yes! to the future through and beyond death; and Yes! to God's everything because God already has provided me with everything. Wonderful!"

C. S. Lewis' description of Narnia in *The Lion, the Witch, and the Wardrobe* is memorable. The wicked witch caused it to always be winter and never Christmas. What a hollow condition of despair. No hope. Empty suffering, much like it would be if there were no resurrection of Jesus, only death and despair. Imagine the hopelessness if Calvary had been the end for Jesus. His final destination, however, was *not* the cross or grave but the resurrection.

Jesus went through the cross and beyond the grave *to get to us*. He is the "first fruits." We are next, intended to be the choice fruit that follows in the wake of the Master. Ours is the choice to surrender in faith, believing that the One to whom we surrender will work newness of life in us according to his will and in his own time and way. Just say "Yes!"[63]

Listen to these words of John Wesley. "Whosoever will reign with Christ in heaven must have Christ reigning with him on earth." Grace and love are central to Christian identity. They yield an optimism of grace, an expectancy that through the power of the Holy Spirit God can and does transform lives, renew churches, and reform societies in ways that more faithfully mirror the life of the coming kingdom of God.

God asks that we open ourselves to life anew, to life at its best. Our answer is to be a simple "Yes!" The kingdom of heaven can reign even now in a human heart and live in faith communities that feature the love of Christ in worship and ministry. This love is to be, can be, must be a present working reality, an active anticipation of heaven below.[64] Just say "YES!"

****

Jesus with the Final Word

(in part a paraphrase of John 11:17-27)

My friends, two critical things are always to be remembered. First, I told my first disciples that I was on my way to Jerusalem knowing full well what religious leaders there were intending to do to me, a horrible crucifixion. My disciples resisted the very idea and urged me to change my travel plans. I didn't. I was faithful to my call because I knew a deep joy that goes beyond this world's tragedy. I was crucified and then, shocking to my not-believing disciples, was actually resurrected. Joy finally spread rapidly.

Second, I announced then what you also must know now. There still is more crucifixion and resurrection ahead. My disciples couldn't really hear this even though I told them more than once. Can you hear me now? Here's a most significant truth. The news isn't just that I would be resurrected. It's also that I *am the resurrection*. My friend Lazarus died and I came and called him forth, explaining to Martha that anyone who believes in me need never die!

Anyone can really live now on earth and then forever far beyond. This is possible by being filled with the very eternal life of my Father. I know that this news was and still is so good that it's hard to believe. Can you believe? Can a divine "YES!" radiate from your very being and be attractive others trapped in a living death? I and my Spirit are saying to you that it can and must be so if you are to be my people in your time. Joy to the world!

12

GO WITH NOTHING?
IT'S RISKY!

J. R. R. Tolkien conceived of a ring of power in his classic work *The Lord of the Rings*. How desperately everyone wanted this ring, including those with noble intentions. The problem was that the ring destroys anyone who keeps it, even the Wise Wizard and the humblest of the Hobbits. Grasping for control will strangle anyone in the end.

Power is not to be pursued. The church of Jesus is to empty itself of reliance on worldly power, taking the form of a suffering servant like Jesus. Members are told by Jesus to go without being loaded down by the supposed assurances of worldly goods. Such traveling lightly is indeed a going out that's risky. Even so, what more does one need if Jesus is always present to supply?

A New York City family was on vacation in their big car. Once in very rural territory, it overtook an Amish buggy pulled by an old horse. A homemade sign on the back of the buggy read, "Energy Efficient Vehicle. Runs on Oats and Grass. Caution--Don't Step in the Exhaust!"

That message is timely for today's Christians. Believers venturing into the world on mission should be cautious about things not only unpleasant on tires but capable of destroying the very integrity of the faith and its mission. When going into the world for Christ, the faithful are to be careful where they drive and what has been packed and taken along.

Leave Money Belts Behind

Surely we should not take along on our Christian missions the deadly sins Mahatma Gandhi once named. He warned against politics without principle, wealth without work, commerce without morality, pleasure without conscience, education without character, science without humanity, and worship without sacrifice. We are to be very careful not to step in these deadly exhausts. They are more dangerous than anything a tired old horse might suddenly produce. By God's grace, we must leave them all behind.[65]

We who believe in Jesus are to lower our worldly expectations about representing a warrior Messiah and the presumed promise of victorious and prosperous lives and churches. Jesus didn't call a host of angels to wipe out the occupying Romans, nor did he leave behind a fortune for his followers to divide among themselves when his earthly end came. He was a poverty-ridden victor.

Jesus wasn't what many in his time and ours have hoped. He was a backwater Savior who sent out a landless group of disciples to go with virtually empty pockets and yet full hearts. They and we are not promised first-class citizenships in this world that supposedly make clear that we serve a generous and rewarding Savior. God's kingdom may be *in* but is not *of* this world!

While mission agents of Jesus might have authority over unclean spirits, they are told to take nothing on their mission journeys except a staff—"no bread, no bag, no money in their belts" (Mk 6:7-13). Granted, bad things might happen along the way and sometimes do. Even so, lowly as they (we) are to be when traveling for our humble and loving Lord, God always promises to be with us to provide what's necessary for our mission. That is, God provides what's needed and not necessarily what's desired.

Disciples of the suffering Master are called to be like him by carrying our own crosses, whatever they turn out to be. That's the negative. Here's the positive. We go into the world as divine agents. Therefore, the promise is that we will be provided with whatever we need for our calling. God is the ultimate and faithful provider.

We won't have whatever we want so that we can appear as the rich kids parading the luxury wares of some big-company executive. We will be given whatever it takes to be faithful and effective disciples of redeeming love. Big titles and salaries aren't among the divine promises. Some suffering likely is.

The Shelter of the Most High

Hear this honest testimony. Are you willing to risk living like this Christian saint? "My Lord God, I have no idea where I am going. I do not see the road ahead of me. I cannot know for certain where it will end, but I believe that the desire to please you does, in fact, please you. And I know that you will lead me by the right road although I may know nothing about it. Therefore, I will trust you always although I may seem to be lost and in the shadow of death. I will not fear because you are ever with me, and you will never leave me alone in the face of my perils."[66]

There's always this good news to take on Christian mission journeys. God will be our "dwelling place in all generations" (Ps 90:1, 91:9). This assurance doesn't promise an easy or carefree existence. Rather, it offers the same assurance that empowered Jesus despite his cross. It's capable of empowering those who follow him and faithfully carry their own crosses (Lk 9:23). God is our home. We dwell in the shelter of the Most High. Living may be in ragged tents, the typical home of pilgrims. Nonetheless, given the divine presence, even these modest dwellings will be quite adequate.

As Christ's followers we must be prepared to believe and proclaim boldly as we go. Proclaim what? Paul identifies the lordship and resurrection of Jesus as the centers of Christian faith and teaching (Rom 10:8-13). We must believe these and show willingness to sacrifice everything for them. Some humiliations are to be endured if necessary. We must give up our pride and good standing in the eyes of others. We are on the world's stage for the applause of only one, our Lord Jesus.

To confess the resurrection of Jesus is to believe in the triumph of love. This makes Christians able to embrace a life not motivated by power or laden with fear or insistent on worldly goods. To confess Jesus as Lord is to affirm that God chose the perfect presence and reflection of himself as an impoverished Southwest Asian man from a backwater of the Roman Empire. To love like Jesus is to reach out graciously and risk as necessary. It's believing that even the world's landless from its backwaters one day can be given citizenship in the Kingdom of Heaven.

To now choose to live and witness in this humbled way requires everything from us believers. Unfortunately, many Christians are forgiven but hardly controlled by the Spirit in all of life. They have never yielded their lives to Jesus *as Lord,* not gone far enough to be caught up in God's mission *on God's terms.* Taking the lordship of Christ seriously means that all of life must come under divine control. With that control comes the authority and ability that will back it up in times of trouble. The luxuries of our neighbors may look good to us. No matter. They never will satisfy nor are they promised to us as a reward for our faithfulness.

There's something toxic about feeding on the world's goods. Daniel refused to eat the rich food of the prevailing empire (Dan 1). The refusal led to his being thrown into a lion's den, and then to the shock and confusion of his captors.

Announced one fully dedicated Christian brother: "Thank God for the Holy Spirit! Thank God for the reality and experience of Pentecost. Thank God that Jesus did not leave us as a powerless, puny, piddling, anemic church for the world! The Holy Spirit is making the Word of God come alive."[67]

Powerful? Yes, but not with superior guns and swords, goods and prestige. Life in the power of the Spirit is the intended life of the church of Jesus.

What the Church Really Needs

The church is to be empowered by the Spirit for its mission. God's power must be at work in us (Eph 3:20). The kingdom of God is not a matter of talk but power (1 Cor 4:20). "More than churches full of people, God wants (and the world needs) *people full of the Spirit*."[68]

We all have personal defense mechanisms. God asks a hard thing, an end to this selfish tendency. The issue is whether we are willing to follow our Lord into threatening territory well beyond our comfort zones. We know that Jesus already has faced and overcome the powers of this world, even death itself. Can we trust him with our fragile lives? We must dare to risk and relax in God's promised care. The church needs people who, in Christ, are relaxing and risking.

Benjamin Franklin once said: "He's a fool that makes his doctor his heir." Why foolishly tempt fate? Why encourage the one who can kill with knowledge of an inheritance waiting in the wings if death were helped along?

We humans often act irrationally, tempting our own self-destruction. Passions of our bodies are allowed to hand disease the keys to our premature deaths. Our nationalisms reach the point of encouraging the world to arm itself with the capacity to annihilate the whole planet. Many people openly defy the God who will be their eternal Judge.

If only we were more conscious of the Great Physician and prepared to benefit from the glorious meanings of our opportunity to be God's heir. Trying to avoid the risks of faith may be the much bigger risk. We willingly lay down now knowing that one day all will be picked up in joy everlasting.

Jonah finally got to Nineveh with God's good news, but only after suffering near tragedy from running the other way. Many believers are anxious to be "saved," rid of sensed guilt, but reluctant to be "sanctified," allowing God to be the real Lord of life.

> Did we in our own strength confide, our striving would be losing,
> Were not the right Man on our side, the Man of God's own choosing:
>
> Dost ask who that may be? Christ Jesus, it is He; Lord Sabaoth His Name,
>
> From age to age the same, *And He must win the battle.*[69]

****

Jesus with the Final Word

(in part a paraphrase of Luke 4:1-13 and John 20:19–31)

It takes more than bread for you to stay alive, my friends. Temptation is around the next corner. Don't be lured by wealth or the glories of "success." Live simply, expectantly, lovingly. I will see that you have all you need. Faithfulness is your business; success is mine.

When on the field of action for me, play for the approval of my Father. The crowd cheers when you manage to beat others as it wishes. However, you are not to be in the beating but the loving and saving business. Remember that being good witnesses of mine shouldn't feature displays of supposed magical abilities or stunning affluence to impress the world's crowds. My Father can be trusted, even when you are caught in the worst of circumstances.

The promise is that nothing can separate you from the love of God (Rom 8:39). Faithfulness to me as your Lord sometimes will send you into danger's path (2 Cor 6:4-10). When in the wilderness, survival will be by my Father's grace and not your self-sufficiency. The wilderness is the place of God's assured presence (Ex 16:9–10), as well as my Father's undeserved but always adequate provision (Ex 16:11–17). Receive my Spirit, stand erect, don't fill your pockets, just go!

13

WHAT DOES "HOLY" LOOK LIKE? LOVE!

I hope that being "holy" as God expects doesn't mean the pure white of flawless performance. That would exclude us all. Rather, it requires shining with the same love that marked the life and death of Jesus. It's a rainbow of beauty and joy, possible only by being *in Christ* and allowing an inner life of the Spirit to be what shines through.

The church for too long has paraded stereotypes of holiness and frustrated believers who want God's best but are aware of their personal limitations. Focus should be shifted to the perfections of God. We are not called to be spotless believers and award-winning performers. We are invited to be love receivers and sharers. This is very possible and most necessary!

The "Holiness Manifesto" is a 2006 document written by fifteen church leaders and scholars, myself included. We were a range of the Wesleyan, Holiness, and Pentecostal traditions of Christianity trying to summarize the heart of Christian holiness values and practices highly relevant to needs of the twenty-first century.

While central to the Bible, holiness isn't a theme to which Christians are readily drawn. There are difficulties of definition and fears of failure. Church leaders have come to new heights of frustration in finding ways to revitalize their congregations and denominations. Something isn't working.

Faith's Essence Is Missing

Church membership in nearly all bodies has flat-lined or declined. The health of churches and the perceived relevance of Christian faith in today's highly secularized culture have been undercut seriously. An serious search has been on for a better method, more effective fad, some newer and bigger program, something that will yield membership growth and commitment.

Christian people in far too many places have fallen prey to a generic Christianity that makes congregations nearly indistinguishable from the general non-Christan culture around them. Churches have come to realize that they need a clear and compelling message that will replace the rusted routines of today's typical church life.

Something truly fresh and attractive is needed, and not just more volume to the music and fun during the after-service attractions. That can be gotten anywhere these days. Lacking is a truly motivating vision of God, a transformational understanding of God's *otherness* on the one hand and of God's *nearness* on the other. Shed must be the obsession with cumbersome religious language, awkward spiritual expectations, and time-consuming programs that are being outdone by the local service clubs and video and audio streams on the internet--to which all church members seem to have regular access.

The faith's essence must be at the center. The message and mission of God, risen in Christ and reigning over all, must be the conscious core of church life. Especially younger people are impatient with artificial compartments, denominations, requirements, and theological divisions that distract and divide believers on human terms. They are tired of building and defending religious institutions designed by and for people long ago.

What is wanted and needed now is a clear message that transcends institutionalism and in-fighting among followers of Jesus. People need to know the unifying power of God that transforms life. Perceiving together the awesomeness of God's holiness is the only thing that can inspire church oneness. What blends and binds faith communities is experiencing together the holy character of a loving God.

God gracefully gives new life that allows reflections of the divine character of love. Such reflecting is holiness, the heart of biblical revelation and the intended center of Christian life. It's the dynamic of effective evangelism. God is holy and calls for a holy people.

God's holy love revealed in Jesus continues yielding life, hope, and salvation.

Only the Spirit of God can draw people into God's holy, loving life. This life delivers from sin, idolatry, bondage, and self-centeredness. It then draws toward a loving service for God, others, and the creation itself.

What Does It Look Like?

When humble enough to receive this transforming love of God, believers become renewed in the image of God as revealed in Jesus. Once empowered by the Spirit of God to be holy people, life proceeds by loving like Jesus. Holy people are loving people. They are not legalistic or judgmental, pursuing a private state of being better than others and demanding the same of others.

Here's what Christian holiness looks like. It's having discovered that "we are not what we can *conquer* but what is *received.*"[70] It's having learned that we were loved long before we could show love. It's knowing that *being* is more important than *having*. We are worth more than the results of our best efforts. Our lives are not positions to be defended but gifts to be shared.

Christian holiness is not flawless performance of religious duties. It's the fulfillment of God's intention for us, life pursued in a selfless manner by the divine law of love. God wants church people to be, think, speak, and act in Christ-like ways. We are to embrace God's urgent call to:

- Be filled with the fullness of God's presence in Jesus Christ;

- Live as forgiven and reconciled in order to be reconciling agents of Jesus;

- Escape individualism by gratefully building accountable communities of Jesus;

- Exercise for the common good the diversity of our divine service gifts;

- Practice compassionate ministries of justice, reconciliation, and peace; and

• Care for the Earth and even the space beyond as good stewards of God's creation.

Christian holiness has gentle textures and attractive colors. They are bright and enlightening and joyful. For too long holiness has been seen like a black-and-white TV sitting in a dingy corner of the house. It doesn't work well because it gets its signal from an old antenna that seems always pointed in the wrong direction.

Believers need to recover the beauty of holiness, the shining joy that flows like rain on a dry and thirsty land. God is anything but dull and boring, life-draining and joy-denying. God exists in living color and wants to paint this color all over our lives. His signal is strong and the programming superior.

The Colors of Love

Divine holiness unfolds with brightness, beauty, joy, gladness, and delight. It fills the heart with song no matter the immediate circumstance. It was this stunning beauty that caused the disciples of Jesus to "consider it all joy" even when they encountered various trials (Jam 1:2). They could embrace suffering as a special kind of glory (Phil 3:10). They could sing in the darkest of times (Acts 16:25).

"Joy to the World" should be more than a popular Christmas carol. It should be the Christian's theme song.[71] Joy is holiness received from above and shared outwardly from a heart in love. The glorious color that shines from God's holiness is the white of pure love. Here is the color of God. "I saw a gold menorah with seven branches, and in the center the Son of Man in a robe and gold breastplate, hair a blizzard of white" (Rev 1:14, *The Message*).

What of us? "Soak me in your laundry and I'll come out clean; scrub me and I'll have a snow-white life. Tune me into foot tapping songs, set these once-broken bones to dancing. Don't look too close for blemishes; give me a clean bill of health" (Ps 51:7). "If your sins are blood-red, they will be snow-white" (Isa 1:18).

A dramatic holiness witness comes from the Apostle Peter. God's divine power has given us everything needed for life and godliness through the knowledge of him who called us by his own glory and goodness. He has given us precious promises so that through them we may escape from the corruption in the world and become participants of the divine nature (2 Pet 1:3–4). How can anything be more dramatic and colorful and joyous than that, being *actual participants* in the divine nature? And what is it? Love!

For this we should live and labor to the benefit of ourselves, the health of our churches, the healing of the nations, and the glory of God. With this perceived and experienced holiness, the church can begin to tremble with an excitement that will make a difference in every aspect of its life and mission. "There is a river whose streams make glad the city of God, the holy place where the Most High dwells. God is within her, she will not fall; God will help her at break of day" (Ps 46:4-5).

Perhaps the public culture of today's Western world is nearing the point when it's ready for the authentic Christian faith to be successfully reintroduced. If so, the lovely and alluring beauty of Christian holiness will need to be at the center. Such has been true in all the great Christian revivals over the centuries.[72]

Holiness is a communal experience, a relational reality. "Even in our weakness, *together* we can be strong, even holy."[73] God's people are his children over all the earth who are experiencing "eternal life" because of their intimate relationship with the Spirit of Jesus. They are to be on a mission of the Spirit of love. Will you join this marvelous mission?

****

Jesus with the Final Word

(in part a paraphrase of Luke 5:1-11)

Hear me, dear friends. I'm calling you to the most important enterprise of all, my Father's mission of redeeming love seeking to cover and convert this world. Be patient with this demanding task and know this. I'll always be close by. I will be encouraging you to keep going, keep believing in the unexpected, having faith in the seemingly impossible, being beautiful because of my Spirit within. When you get frustrated, don't focus on threatening failure. In my kingdom, frustration is only the front door. Participating in my Father's very life of love makes the difference.

I realize that seeing me on the cross was devastating to the faith of my first followers. How could the true Messiah be so humiliated by this world? It would take my resurrection to realize that what was seen on the cross was not the triumph of this world's power. It was a presentation of the amazing power of the love my Father has for lost humankind. That awful death of mine was completely voluntary and totally for you. It was a dramatic picture of who my Father really is.

Sacrificial love will stand for all eternity. Receive this amazing gift and be its beautiful representatives. Be holy light in action in your time. The world in which you minister is full of violence and death. Your role is to be and share the larger truth. Death soon will itself be dead. Injustice will be reversed. Love alone will prevail!

14

SHOULD SOME CHRISTIAN VOICES SHUT UP? YES!

I know this question seems rude. Forgive me, but I mean it. Some voices keep shouting alarming information that surprises even God. What qualifies us to leave the simple gospel of God in Christ and start announcing wisdom previously unknown until we came along? The problem goes beyond rash talking to too much sitting.

All talk and no action is an easy way to go in the Christian community. We receive saving grace and then mostly sit in a pew on Sundays and enjoy our lack of guilt. The Book of James was thought by Martin Luther to be an "epistle of straw" because of its stress on "works." This New Testament book, however, does this because it knows that faith without works is dead. If a believer brags on faith and never really does anything about it, it's time to shut up!

Sorry for the harsh words, but no apology is warranted. Such a "shut up" is in the Bible, and even sharper words for the church. Religion easily can become its own worst enemy. Believers can allow themselves to become so dazzled by God's majesty and power, so intoxicated by God's wondrous love that they speculate about things far beyond their actual ability to know and do. Sometimes we believers become paralyzed by paradise. We can be so praise oriented that we are action anemic.

Praising God is foundational. Even so, believers also must hear carefully Paul defending himself to the Corinthians. There's a compulsion in the gospel of Christ that demands active follow-through. While love is full of freedom and releases the believer from the binding of law, it doesn't include permission to fail by doing nothing with the love but enjoy it privately.

Shout Out or Shut Up!

To be blessed by God requires becoming a blessing to others. We who claim to be followers of Jesus are thereby called to be doing something with what God in Christ has done for us. We must be acting faithfully or we should stop spilling out our empty words of praise for God.

Recall these words of John Henry Newman: "I sought to hear the voice of God and climbed the topmost steeple, but God declared, 'Go down again, I dwell among the people'." Hear well and be thankful, of course. However, then the thankfulness also go down and serve the One who has spoken so graciously.

To hear and fail to go down is to sour and finally obstruct the marvelous message heard from above. Faith without related works is dead, even disgusting to God. That was made brutally clear long ago (Amos 5:21-24). Be careful about inviting Amos to your church as a guest speaker.

Psalm 147 begins and ends in the same way, praising God. The God who created the world also continues to rule it actively. The psalmist suggests three typical actions of God. There is *gathering* the outcasts, *lifting* the downtrodden, and *casting* the wicked to the ground. God is more than just the distantly reigning divine being. God acts out of his being because of the loving nature of his being.

This is a key lesson for believers who are tempted to claim the faith without proclaiming it to others, benefitting from the faith without sharing its benefits with others. The love of God, and thus the children of God, are to gather, lift, and cast down.

The people of Israel, long stuck in foreign exile, had begun to give up, thinking they had been abandoned by God (Isa 40:27). The prophet Isaiah vigorously refutes this thought, parading a series of verbs of God's actions to the contrary. Here are verbs believers should always keep in mind.

God "sits" above the heavens and yet does more than sit. God stretches, spreads, brings, makes, and redeems. No earthly ruler can withstand long the powerful actions of God who insists on being in action. Exile was deserved but would not be forever. The Jewish exiles, while exhausted and powerless, should not have lost faith because fainting and sleeping are never among God's actions.

What Are We To Do?

One divine action is granting undeserved grace and fresh power to those who are fainting. Another is ensuring that justice finally will be done. God always follows through, as must we who claim special relationship with God. Receiving requires sharing. Being blessed calls for action out of the blessing. This is possible because God "gives power to the faint and strengthens the powerless" (Isa 40:29). Once strengthened, God's people are to act in several ways.

We are to "mount up with wings like eagles, run and not be weary, walk and not faint" (Isa 40:31). We are to activate the grace of God on behalf of ourselves and others. We may be like "grasshoppers" (vs. 22) in comparison to the God "who sits above the circle of the earth," but we are loved grasshoppers now enabled to jump with joy!

Christian people must be healed of dreaded disease of theological amnesia so that we remember who God really is and thus, by God's grace, who we should be in divine service.

> Open my mouth, and let me bear,
> gladly the warm truth ev'rywhere;
> Open my heart and let me prepare
> love with Thy children thus to share.[74]

As the Hebrew prophets crassly put it: "Shout out or shut up!"

The psalmist invokes God to bring our senses to bear in testimony to his work (Ps 119). Open *my eyes* is a challenge to be still and observe God's activity so that our witness will be deeply grounded and properly activated. Each verse of this psalm begins with a different human organ—eyes, ears, mouth, each called to attentive witness to what God is doing in us and now intends to do through us. It's all shared with us so that we are enabled to live holy and productive lives before God and for others.

Christians often have avoided social engagement of their faith witness. In contrast to the aggressive 19th-century Christian advocacy for the abolition of slavery, the elevation of women's rights, and urgently needed economic reforms, many believers were sidelined during the civil rights movement of the 1950s and 1960s. The very people who should have been pressing the principles of Christian faith into culture were silent behind firewalls of defensiveness and fear. They feared a theological "liberalism" might lead to spiritual capitulation.

Now we must shake off the obsession with eliminating differences among ourselves. Sameness is not our Christian goal. Expanding the Kingdom of God is. We believers are not necessarily to all look, speak, and act exactly alike. Let's face the inevitable diversity within the church and fearlessly get to work with differences seen as a resource and not an obstruction![75]

Paul testifies to doing all for the sake of the gospel so that he could share in its blessings (1 Cor 9:23). Granted, we believers don't gain our salvation by earning it through any doing of our own. Even so, we who really are in Christ naturally will be doing the things of Christ or risking the loss of our salvation.

We must be free in Christ, but cautiously and lovingly in action with our freedom. We must shut up when it comes to boasting about our "rights" that are hurtful to others. We are to speak out when necessary to make clear that Christ's love makes us both free and "slaves" of Christ rendering enthusiastic service to others (Eph 6:6).

Here's how to be really strong. "To the weak I became weak so that I might win the weak" (1 Cor 9:22). Paul was obligated to deliver the good news in Christ. "Woe to me if I don't!" (1 Cor 9:16). If I won't act like Christ, then I should shut up about Christ! We must be healed of our theological amnesia so that we can remember who God really is and who, by God's grace, we can and should be in his service. Here's a prayer that ought be on the lips of all believers:

> Dear God, please keep my churchgoing from being painful to you. I know the church too often functions offensively in your eyes. Your prophets have addressed this directly on many occasions. Whatever has our attention tends to have all of us. Praising God with all our hearts is a high calling indeed. Still, it's not the only calling. Getting stuck in the praise posture without following through finally leads you to telling us to shut up, get out, start over. May that consequence not be so for me!

Faith without related works is dead—and disgusting to God.

John Wesley was right. Our abiding concern should be to preserve the two truths that are co-definitive of real Christianity. Without God's grace we *cannot* be saved; without our grace-empowered but uncoerced participation in God's mission, God's grace *will not* save. Follow through or faith has failed.

Accountability is tough love that encourages frequent reflection on how well or poorly life in Christ is going.[76] Unfortunately, many who profess new life in Jesus Christ have little or no spiritual accountability. John Wesley was an enthusiast for small groups of Christian accountability. His "class meetings" saw to it that participants stayed the course, continued in Christ, and became rooted and increasingly built up and strengthened in the faith (Col 2: 6-7).[77]

Is this happening where you worship and serve? We must grow up in the faith or eventually have to shut up about how grand it is.

****

Jesus with the Final Word

(in part a paraphrase of Mark 1:29-39)

Please give this important word real attention my friends. Let me recount scenes from one day in my public ministry. They are good examples that make one important point. I healed a mother-in-law and soon she "began serving." She was anxious to put her wellness to work. I tried to stop people from spreading false impressions of the reasons for my coming. They were sharing nothing but excitement about the drama of my healings. They wouldn't stop picturing me in ways other than I wished. I occasionally sought a place of prayer, just needing to get away. My disciples urged me to return to the applauding crowds to dazzle them some more.

I urge you to minister in love, but don't dazzle for attention. Preachers of my gospel need to focus on my real identity and not encourage people to get carried away with the alluring externals. Any who do get carried away with their own exciting agendas need to change their attitudes and actions or just shut up!

You are to teach and act so that the bigger context comes clear to people. That context is their knowing who I am, why I came, and what their action obligations are. Otherwise, it's better that you just be quiet. Granted, even when you are completely faithful to my charge to humility, things won't always work out as they should. They certainly didn't for me. Your obligation nonetheless is to do all you can and then leave the rest to my Father. Don't take charge to build your own reputations. Take time out to rest your mouth and grow in holiness.

15

BEYOND "QUID PRO QUO"? DEFINITELY!

This question requires a Latin refresher. *Quid pro quo* means that we expect *a favor for a favor*. You scratch my back and I'll scratch yours. I'll take an eye for an eye and a tooth for a tooth. Evil brings punishment, evil for evil; good brings reward, good for good.

This human thinking and acting, sometimes mentioned and illustrated in the Bible, usually is condemned. How to avoid acting this very human way is the big question. We are to love without expectation of reward. When violated, we are to avoid thinking that revenge is appropriate. If judgment really is deserved, leave it to the divine Judge who takes everything into consideration and always is fully just.

Are we people of Jesus clever enough to work with the aggressive capitalists of the world? Can we manage to avoid doing God's work in the world's way? Churches that become big business operations and turn large amounts of money annually are tempted to go astray in their non-spiritual affairs. Are there non-spiritual things or is everything believers do to be thought of spiritually?

The Business of God's House

Solomon built a magnificent temple in Jerusalem as a house for God. Supposedly wise or not, read 1 Kings 5 and 9 closely and note how Solomon went wrong. David's son got hacked and he hacked back. Hiram, King of Tyre, was big in the lumber business and could cut quite a deal. Solomon got in the riddle business and cut back as best he could.

Is this hack-for-a-hack how temples and churches are to be built? God's people always have faced the daunting task of being special people in an ungodly world. We are to be and do *as God is and does*. Love hardly endorses our championing of *quid pro quo* business ethics.

Shouldn't faithfulness bring privileges? Don't good people deserve good and bad people get what's coming to them? Aren't "pacifists" weak people who aren't prepared to deal with the strong by necessary opposing strength? Was Jesus having a bad day when he told people to turn the other cheek? Doesn't such turning encourage more evil and let the guilty skip deserved punishment? Shouldn't everyone get what they deserve? Shouldn't "holy" people get even when justified? Is getting even ever justified?

The psalmist asks, "If we were good, my just Lord, then give us good in return, the good we deserve. God will do good to those who are good" (Ps 25:4). Surely there is a clear link between God's goodness and the material prosperity and safety of God's faithful ones. Or is there? The Bible strongly puts forward the concept of divine *grace,* meaning a person being given a goodness not deserved and that couldn't be earned. There are various Bible verses that counterbalance the view expressed in Psalm 25:4.

The Book of James goes to the heart of this matter. Does anyone believe in our glorious Lord Jesus Christ while showing favoritism to the people who show up at church dressed smartly and giving no evidence of ability to expand the congregation's budget? The right answer is blunt. Showing such partiality is committing sin (Jam 2:9).

Mercy must be greater than preference shown because of social status and likely favorable returns. There will be no mercy shown to the merciless (vs. 13). God's mercy flows our way because of our faith and faithfulness and nothing else. Our achievements don't add up to the size of our homes and bank accounts. Jesus finished his earthly life with hardly any clothing left. Did he deserve more?

Why was Amos so hard on God's people (8:4-7)? It was because they had allowed themselves to become a big part of the problem. Those representing God must engage the world without being captured by it and trying to mirror it to church advantage. Jesus people must not use smoke screens and dirty tricks as ways of turning people in Christ's direction and increasing income.

Wrong methods usually lead to wrong results even when employed for good purposes. Still, church people have to be smart in dealing with conspiring opposition or the gospel message will never get the hearing it deserves. It's a delicate line to walk. The church must function in the world without the world quietly functioning in the church.

A rich man caught his manager cheating clients for his own gain (Lk 16:1-13). Jesus condemned the wrong while also commending the cleverness involved. The man had figured out ways to pull off his twisted scheme. By implication, Christians must be smart without using quick wits for wrong purposes. The man always was looking for an edge, and Jesus people must be looking for opportunities not to cheat but to bless.

When on the streets, one must know the streets. There's an unavoidable risk in being involved closely with sinners. The problem is that not being with them and knowing them well limits greatly the ability to win them for God's kingdom. The evangelist must take care not to be dragged down by the one being evangelized.

Is Being Clever "Worldly"?

Are we Christians inevitably parts of evil social systems that regularly practice favoritism? Aren't we participants without giving it any thought. Christians know that a few are reaping great profit at the expense of others. Maybe we aren't able to change this complex business. Must we be part of it?

We seem too busy arguing over the class and creed distinctions maintained among ourselves inside the church to even try engaging the larger issues outside. Hopefully we won't be judged for not changing what we thought we couldn't. Social Security, investment, and retirement funds are handled by unknown others, often for unknown purposes. Is there an option?

Self-centered people have ghetto tendencies. We build social boxes, live inside them, and view with suspicion and even hatred those outside. Even in the church, sometimes there appear to be closed systems around particular interpretations of Scripture and preferred spiritual experiences. This makes church unity in diversity almost impossible. Who's responsible? Can we be "clever" enough to find ways around such hurtful business? Is bring clever "worldly"?

It's urgent that we who believe in Jesus Christ allow the Spirit of Christ to review our inner motivations and sharpen our social engagements. It's hard to act without expecting something in return. We need a better path of life that dares to act rightly for its own sake, not for some return we think we will deserve.

Quid pro quo must be resisted. Jesus people are never to live with the mindset of getting even when given the short end of the stick. That doesn't mean that evil should be tolerated passively as though it's inevitable and irresistible. "The Lord is good, a stronghold in a day of trouble; he protects those who take refuge in him. Repay no one evil for evil. If possible, so far as it depends on you, live peaceably with all" (Rom 12:17-18).

We who claim to serve Jesus have a subtle and fatal tendency. It's quietly replacing God in church life with ourselves and our private agendas. We want to do God's things, yes, but *in our own way*. Pride was thought quite acceptable by secular singer Frank Sinatra. He crooned, "I've lived a life that's full, I've traveled each and every highway. And more, much more than this, *I did it my way*." That may be Frank and the world in general, but God says, "This isn't to be the way for my people!"

There Is a Jesus Way

Jesus is *the way*, truth, and life. For the Christian, there is to be no *my way*. If God's people, on whom God has showered love and grace, insist on going their own way to their own "deserved" advantage, their fate will be this. God will allow them to do as they wish and eventually pay the high price they will deserve. Christians must be part of a disciplined community of faith, a new creation determined to do things *God's way*. It's the way of reconciliation, not revenge and expected returns.[78]

The issue is expected returns. There can be no "using" people for church gain. Any abuse of people is by definition church loss. There, however, surely can be wise investments in legitimate causes for fair gain, which then is put to proper church use. Good stewardship is part of good discipleship.

Reconciliation is the process of the love of God moving against the ghettos of exclusion and discrimination and expected paybacks now deserved. How can it be known that we who believe in Jesus actually are disciples of Jesus? One way is that we have reconciling tendencies displaying self-sacrificing love for each other (Jn 13:35). Jesus people are to be insisting on building bridges that link people instead of walls that keep undesirables away.

The people of God's Spirit are to be living models of a coming new world, the kingdom of God, created only by the reconciling grace of God. The church can become a compass for a disoriented world *only if* it embraces the qualities that exemplify good evangelism that's surrounded with hospitality, enabling relationships, and integrity of intention. These are to combined into a reconciling message of good news, doing good for good's sake and not personal or church profit.

This sort of community evangelism is part of the good news. It shows a people who are for the welfare of other people and not for mere community gain in return. "What does the Lord require of you, but to do justice, love kindness, and walk humbly with your God" (Mic 6:6-8). If there needs to be judgmental fire on anyone, God will send it rather than the church trying to set it.

The fate of evildoers is God's business, not ours (Deut 32:35, Rom 12:19, Heb 10:30). Unlike us, God never takes vengeance from impure motives. "Do not seek revenge or bear a grudge, but love your neighbor as yourself." (Lev 19:18). There is only one just Judge, and it isn't us. Jesus people are to follow the Lord's command to love even enemies and pray for them who persecute (Matt 5:44), leaving any justified vengeance to God.[79]

Holiness for Christians is God's empowerment that enables living above our selfish instincts. *Quid pro quo* is what we sometimes wrongly wish. As the sky soars high above the earth, so God works in ways far above how we often think and work. God chose the overlooked and exploited. Now the chosen nobodies are to expose the hollow pretensions of the supposed somebodies and not act like them for personal vindication or gain (Isa 55:9, 1 Cor 1:27-29).

****

Jesus with the Final Word

(in part a paraphrase of Mark 7:24-30)

I wasn't having a bad day when I said one should turn the other cheek. Returning evil for evil only increases the evil. My being nailed to the cross was hardly justice. I could have called a crowd of angels to slaughter my killers, but that wouldn't have furthered the doing of my Father's saving and redeeming will.

You don't deserve my Father's grace because you have the right credentials or have done some good things. Here are three Latin words you must not mimic—*quid pro quo*. Don't seek to nail people because they nailed me. My healings of the Syro-Phoenician woman and the deaf and mute man involved people outside the religious community of my people. They were candidates for my healing only because of their unusual faith.

I tested the woman by being blunt about giving the children's food to dogs. She came right back by throwing Isaiah 49:6 in my face, and she was right. To whom is the love of my Father offered? "I'm setting you up as a light for the nations." You qualify for forgiving grace not because you are children of Abraham or are a member of the right church. You qualify because you are a beloved creation of my Father who is willing to be the redeeming light. The poor appeared at the door of my emergency room with no insurance cards in hand, just great needs and belief that I could and would help. I could and did. Be my agents of selfless love and do the same.

16

HOW CAN WE BE UNITED?
BE HOLY!

Jesus said that God's Spirit was upon him to launch a new creation. Pentecost was an outpouring of the Spirit on the newly constituted church of Jesus. It was an amazing new-creation reality. The crowd in Jerusalem on that dramatic day was made up of people from many nations. Each somehow heard and understood the gospel proclamation in his or her own language.

God's intent is universal redemption, a tower of redeeming love, potentially the home for a reunited humanity. Meanwhile, the church of Jesus should be a visible example of the unity possible in Christ. How is this unity possible despite the great diversity of believers? It's possible only by each member having the same Spirit of Christ within. Real Christian unity is enabled by real holiness shared by all members, different though they may be otherwise.

Paul explains that life "in the Spirit" and "led by the Spirit" is a fresh state of human existence in sharp contrast to living "according to the flesh" and "under the law." One role of the Spirit of Jesus today is building up the church in unity.

The Genesis story in chapter eleven is about a human tower that's an edifice of pride and power. The new Spirit tower, the church, is to be the reverse, a worldwide family of the humbled redeemed. It's to be offering true community for all people willing to join.

In the church, all are to be gladly recognized and valued as equally loved children of God and members of the Body of Christ. Being holy together is being one in Christ regardless of skin color, ethnic identity, or national origin.

A Pentecost People

To be Pentecost people in this world requires having been in an upper room where divine fire falls and hearts are set ablaze. That fire dissolves mere religion. Authentic spirituality emerges and the uniting life of God's community begins to shine. The good news is that Jesus, having died on the cross and risen from the dead, dies no more. He now sits at the right hand of the Father and has become for us, for *all of us*, the life-giving Spirit (1 Cor 15:45). New lives of love and unity emerge![80] Our prayer together becomes:

> Finish then Thy new creation,
> Pure and spotless let us be;
> Let us see Thy great salvation,
> Perfectly restored in Thee.[81]

The Bible reports that once there was Babel, a tower of human pride and ambition (Gen 11). Now under construction is a tower of God's Spirit, the church as God's community of reconciliation. In Babel there is a clutter of conflicting and unintelligible voices. By contrast, the church is to be a unifying new community that rises above all narrow human tribes, nations, races and denominations.

Pentecost is the Spirit's recreating presence gifting believers and blending them together into one redeemed family worldwide. It's the church being built by the loving Spirit of God who unites rather than discriminate, isolate, or divide. God is building a community that gladly embraces all people who are embraced by God and have accepted this redeeming grace.

Out of many is to be emerging an amazing oneness, the church of Jesus. It's an inclusive rather than exclusive community. It's God's alternative to our tribalistic tendencies. It can be erected only by the initiative and holy, unifying grace of God. Disciples belong to this new community of the Spirit when choosing to follow the risen Jesus. They are partners in replacing the old Babel tower, builders together of the tower of love, the family of God.

Holiness and Unity

A "holiness movement" in the late nineteenth century sought fresh spiritual life for believers, and then through them a reinvigorating of their church affiliations. Unfortunately, in the midst of this reforming enthusiasm and occasional narrowness, some proceeded to further organizational disunity with the formation of their own new denominations. Too often these were built around personalities or particular doctrinal or practice perspectives with little regard for the larger disunity picture and its negative impact on world evangelism.

Jesus prayed for both the holiness *and* the unity of his disciples (Jn 17). Can holiness unite instead of divide? The twentieth century saw major Christian unity efforts worldwide, the "ecumenical" movement. "Holiness" people tended to stand on the sidelines of these efforts, concerned about motivations and the doctrinal depth of the many unity attempts. A significant alternative today is the emergence of the Wesleyan Holiness Connection with its motivation and address being *holinessandunity.org*.[82]

There remains a near universal acceptance of the ideal of Christian unity and a discomfort with the mission implications of the church's significant separateness. Some holiness leaders have regarded "sectism" as sin and "perfect love" as the only escape from rampant division in the church. They have envisioned Christianity as a visible fellowship of all the "saints" united in spite of the diversity among them. A passionate concern for personal "sanctification" should not eliminate an equally great concern for the united integrity of the fellowship of all believers.[83]

One deeply concerned holiness brother was very active with the "Faith and Order" division of the ecumenical movement in the United States. Here are two of the many benefits he saw flowing from such involvement. Participation is an opportunity to learn *about* and *from* other Christian traditions, including elements of Christian faith that may lie dormant in one's own tradition. It also provides opportunity for partnership in important theological exploration, relationship building, and mission efforts.[84]

This brother admits to times of frustration in the uniting effort, but still concludes that "the benefits far outweigh the liabilities." The biggest benefit is taking one small step toward fulfillment of our Lord's prayer that "we may all be one" in order that "the world may believe." Seeking unity among believers is an attempt to respond positively to Paul's plea for believers to "lead lives worthy of our calling, making every effort to maintain the unity of the Spirit in the bond of peace" (Eph 4:1-3).

Being together *in Christ* (unity in holiness) is the only source of the viability of the church's oneness. It's the only path to the practical possibility of a united even though highly diverse faith community. In Christ, all things are held together (Col 1:17b) and all people are to be valued equally. The church is intended to be the unique held-together community of Christ's disciples.

The church's unity is to be in Christ *by Christ's Spirit*. Christ is the primary unifying subject and the Spirit is the primary unifying dynamic. It's to be one body regardless of its various racial and national origins and the wide range of its thinking and practices on numerous secondary issues. All members participating in the eternal life of God (holiness) are sharing the same Spirit life and thus are one with each other regardless of differences otherwise.

Unity in Diversity

The church must champion the vision of its essential oneness while also celebrating and being enriched and not impeded by its inevitable diversities. The disciples of Jesus are called to model before a badly divided world the beauty and peace of a truly united human community in Christ. Failure here is a great danger to the success of the church's world mission.

Christian identity and church membership are to be closely related. They both are to be rooted in Christian spiritual experience, persons being transformed into the image of Christ by action of the Spirit. Affiliation with a church body apart from new life in Christ is false church membership, poor theology, and a threat to mission.

To be oriented to the presence and work of the Spirit is not to be mired in subjectivism that creates anarchy in church life. Spirit orientation is the conscious determination of Christian believers to be free of artificial and forced structures of belief and church life. Being committed together to serious discipleship enables a credible covenant community and thus effective world outreach.

The Bible makes clear that the Creator is determined to *re-create* and *re-unite*. Cooperating with God's fresh activity helps make the divine newness possible. Jesus embodied what we lost humans needed so badly, *God with us* in human flesh for our salvation. Jesus was God's newness on full display. Even more is now ahead. Jesus has prayed that his body, the church, will be united and actively about his Father's ongoing mission. May it be so!

****

Jesus with the Final Word

(in part a paraphrase of John 17:20-26)

There's a crucial mandate facing my people, my church. You will be in and seeking to minister to a very broken and divided world. You must attend to your own oneness in my love, and only then address the world in a way it can believe. As I am one with my Father, may you all be one with each other because of the wonderful ministry of my gifting and unifying Spirit.

You, all my loved disciples, are very different from each other. Nonetheless, don't allow that to fragment your fellowship or abort your mission. The differences must become a resource for mission and not an obstacle to its success. Face it, my friends. You will never all see alike on everything or be organized into a single earthly church institution. My concern is not merged institutions and uniformity of all perspectives and practices. My concern is *spiritual unity*. What you must do is *be* alike as serious children of my Father. Only in that spiritual commonness will you find true unity. The needed life transformation into lives of holiness can only happen through the blending miracle of my richly relational Spirit.

Everything critical in the life of my church is born and should hold together in ways reflective of the relationship between myself and my Father. As we are one, may my church become one. You will be one with each other only as you are all living truly *in me* and seeking to minister *by my Spirit*. Your individual relationships with me are what make you a spiritual family. Be humbly reconciled and active reconcilers. Help my people be known as the hope of the world and not seemingly more of its problem!

Once our nagging questions about God have been addressed, we naturally ask this. Given who God is, what is the life that can be for us? Love and Holiness are keys since they are essential aspects of God's nature and central expectations of who we are to be as God's redeemed children. Dare we be Radical, Risky, and United as we choose to do things God's way? Jesus always is given the last word!

17

WHY WRITE YOUR STORY? WITNESS!

Recording one's own life story isn't necessarily an exercise in personal arrogance. One surely hopes, as the sarcastic comment goes, it isn't the most popular form of fiction! We humans do like to think the best of ourselves and tend to remember what we like most about who we've been over the years.

However, looking back and seeing how God has been showing the way and making things possible can identify a life's wisdom, a story deserving of sharing with others. Leaving behind a few life markers might help the next generation stay on course. We Christians are called to testify and often we can do that best by telling what we know best, our own stories. We had been lost until found by a loving God!

Of course, autobiography can be so much fiction. It also can be a means of telling the biggest spiritual truths we have come to know. What has altered and directed our years? Can we recall and record without being self-serving? We may skip over a few negatives and highlight the biggest positives. We also, by God's grace, may come to understand in hindsight what was not evident at the time. It's good to think back so that others may be helped to see forward.

Earth or Ocean?

I heard this as the twenty-first century was about to begin. "Only when we saw our planet from space did we humans realize that we should not have called it *Earth*. We should have called it *Ocean*." About seventy percent of this planet is covered by water, much of it very deep, with virtually all of this vast liquid world still unexplored by humans.

As an aging person freshly viewing our past for the first time from this elevated vantagepoint, what should we be called? Who have we been really? Grandchildren deserve our best effort. The need to know our reality may go much farther than that. Let's remember and share, not knowing for how many and for how long our story might linger.

When a person begins to ponder the life that has been, thoughts are only modest probings beneath a vast surface of what was not all conscious at the time, not now fully remembered, and likely never to be totally understood. Bits and pieces are brought to the surface and a story takes shape, maybe the story we want to be known. Even so, God will help if we honestly try. In fact, God may be found at the story's very center, something we hadn't quite realized before. Our planning across the years may have been only a small part of a larger plan we haven't quite seen until now.

Signatures and Markings

My personal autobiography is now in its fourth published edition, presumably the last.[85] It's not that I've kept changing my mind. New things kept happening, I lived longer than expected, and for some reason the publishers were willing to keep spending the money.

Life is influenced greatly by the contexts in which it's lived and the stories and beliefs that set its direction and capture its understood meanings. An autobiography is an attempt to unravel these stories, retell them well, and witness to their underlying beliefs. For me, the shaping contexts have included tales of immigration, war, hunting and fishing, camp meetings, a pioneering church reform movement, the history of several university campuses and congregations, the wonderful love of two wives, the presence of children, grandchildren, and now great-grandchildren, and especially the revelation of one supreme life in which I have believed and sought to follow. It's the story of Jesus.

An autobiography seeks to pull everything together in a way that charts past meaning and future destiny. It's a daring to step. Who was I? Who should I have been? What mountains have I been on and what if anything did I see as I looked from their heights? What about others? I have been privileged to help some others do life reflecting as they allowed me to be their biographer.[86]

Since I'm running for no political office at my advanced age, I assume that my prime motive for writing my own autobiography was charting the long life I've lived and capturing the most important ideas I've had and now have evaluated carefully. The motive has been to gain no advantage, only to discover and share the wisdom gained in one lifetime. I merely have wanted to advocate for what I think is true and important for others when I'm off the scene.

Gloria Gaither tells her story and that of her husband Bill by highlighting the wonderful life of Someone else they had met (Jesus).[87] I now have joined these two valued friends in this same treasured discovery. Our human history finally can be a discovery of *His*-Story, the divine one who has surrounded and infused our days with love.

If such surrounding and infusing is real, then surely one has an obligation to pay attention to the flow of these things, reconsider the road now traveled, and look back for the distinctive marks of God etched into our paths. Others may come along and benefit from an awareness of how the road got there in the first place and how God once directed some people in ways that prepared the way for others.

The alumni magazine of Anderson University is called *Signatures*. One outstanding autobiography is titled *Markings*.[88] In the New Testament, the four Gospels are the several tellings of the one story of Jesus. The Book of Acts is a recounting of the actions of the early Christian apostles that in fact were the activities of the Spirit of Christ through them. Knowing one's beginnings often is key to understanding one's pathways and endings. Studying the early church is critical for the wisdom of today's church.

Giants on My Path

To tell a life story is a good means of expressing indebtedness and sharing one's ongoing faith witness. To forget is to sever a key link with trans-generational identity and meaning. Because of God's grace over the years, remembering can be reason for rejoicing and impacting the coming years of others. The biblical tradition rests heavily on the significance of such memory. The very process of my writing activity has disciplined me to remember and increased my awareness of God's having been moving in my life all along, even if unseen at the time.

Who am I? I've been trying to get that clarified. I've recorded my central memories as a family man and "theologian," one who understands his ministry to have been a pilgrim thinker working on behalf of a pilgrim people. It's been an attempt at "testimony" for the sake of the future. It's worth taking time to remember and tell the stories of God in our yesterdays. It's like "sending a nighingale into the air and hoping that it's song will never be forgotten."[89]

When completing my biography of John S. Pistole, then president of Anderson University and previously a national leader in public service, I had no doubt that his life story deserved being told. What caused me to respond to his request to be the biographer was his expressed motivation. John's concern was Christian witness and not personal ego. This troubled world would be much better off if there were many more giants like John who, by God's grace, have crossed my path and enriched my walking.

Then came Kevin W. Mannoia, another giant on my path. The motivation for his story being told was much like John's, Christian witness. That's again why I agreed to research and write his life story (*Anchored and Reaching*). I'm honored to have played a small role in being sure that these life stories aren't forgotten. It's the sacred task of archiving great Christian testimonies.

I've recorded other life stories, including Lillie S. McCutcheon (*She Came Preaching*), Daniel S. Warner (*It's God's Church!*), Clark H. Pinnock (*Journey Toward Renewal*), James Earl Massey (*Aspects of My Pilgrimage*), and Robert H. Reardon (*Staying on Course*). These are precious memories, lives very well lived, deep Christian footprints in the sands of time. The very book titles point our way ahead.

The purpose of recording of my own life has been much the same (*A Pilgrim's Progress*). It was not to draw attention to myself, likely not worth much of your time, but to show how God graciously works in the course of our living, believing, and serving, enabling a simple pilgrim like me to progress. If that's been true in my humble circumstances, and it has been, then it also can be true for you in yours, however humble the setting might be.

I resonate with this characterization of me once announced to a crowd by a scholar friend. "Dr. Callen is a creative catalyst on the progressive side of the middle of the theological spectrum." That seems about right. I have cherished deep roots that make possible fresh fruit. I'm an historian by instinct and training, as can be seen in many of my books. I want future generations to be aware of the wisdom that helped make possible my yesterdays.

I'm a flexible conservative, maybe even a recovering fundamentalist who's been privileged to stand on many strong shoulders. I hope that the modest footprints I leave in the sand will guide someone in the future to some good places. The several short essays in this book's collection are intended to further this sharing and guiding purpose. They are what I consider bits of wisdom discovered on my journey and now offered for your consideration.

Like my teacher David Elton Trueblood, I have done the remembering and writing while I could.[90] Will you remember yours? Hope that these words come true. "

****

Jesus with the Final Word

(in part a paraphrase of Luke 3:7-18)

Be careful about the face you wear in public, my friends. A shallow smile will not suffice for my agents in this world. Facial appearances can be very misleading. A child of God by my Father's grace isn't to manage only a modest grin just to make a good impression. Even kids see through such false faces. If you choose to follow me, you can find and experience a real joy that reflects the actual coming of God into your life. The truly happy face comes from the depths of a happy heart.[91] When you have found the depths, share the joy with others.

People are attracted to the authentic and mock the hypocrite. It's time to put out the trash to be burned. The fire will be my Spirit coming and cleansing. Your relationships with my Father must give evidence of more than conformity to any law. Obvious must be the fruit of life in my Spirit (Gal 5:22-23). That fruit is luscious, life-sustaining, and joy-producing, great material for testifying to others about the sheer marvel of divine grace.

People like Tiberius, Pilate, and Herod often are thought to be the ones who made world history. When it came time for God to make history, however, the divine Word came to none of these supposed greats. The outcasts of society were selected to receive and carry the good news that arrived in my birth in the most modest of places. I'm talking about those shepherds near Bethlehem and the fishermen I recruited along the shores of Lake Galilee, and now you whoever and wherever you are. Receive my coming and begin to change the world! Then record it all for the future guidance of others.

18

CALL ME "CHRISTIAN"? NO!

Presumed identity does matter. Reputation and potential influence are linked closely in the public eye. I have a preference about mine. Don't misunderstand. I'm not jumping the ship of faith. I'm just hoping for a more neutral label over the door. The Christian past has too much unholy baggage for me to be happily labeled "Christian" today.

How about something like "Follower of Jesus"? He needs no defence, requires no awkward explanations for the wounds he's inflicted on human history (there are none). I haven't left the church. I just want her to be more like Jesus and known that way. I hope the same for myself and want to be known for being a pilgrim on the sacred journey of following Jesus.

It might seem surprising, even a little shocking for a senior minister with a range of Christian credentials, but it shouldn't be. I haven't abandoned my Christian faith and converted to something new and strange. To the contrary, the living of life, coupled with my long experience in the fields of Christian theology and church history, have deepened my faith. It's just that it also has brought me some cautionary lessons. I no longer can assume that everything called "Christian" represents the world's greatest wisdom.

Not a New Religion

The Christian church isn't all she should be and never has been. One result is this. There's lots of baggage in church history and I'd people to stop thinking that it all represents me. I respectfully request that I not be called "Christian" in public. That raises too many questions and requires too many explanations and cautious footnotes. I aspire to the best of identities (Acts 11:26; Eph 2:19–20). Unfortunately, some people, programs, and institutions associated with the name "Christian" are far from ideal.

Was Jesus a Jew? Of course. What kind of Jew? Was he a Pharisee, Sadducee, Zealot, Essene, or some other segment of Judaism in his day? As far as we know, he loved them all, at times was severely critical of each for different reasons, but formally never belonged to any. He hadn't come to destroy his beloved tradition or pick one branch over another. He came to reform them all in fundamental ways. Identifying exclusively with any one of the "traditions of the elders" was not an acceptable option for him. Jesus was something very new and different.

This favor I'm asking was inspired by some recent reading.[92] The suggestion put forward was to be called a "follower of Jesus" rather than a "Christian." This preference rests on what I consider some good reasons. One is that "Christianity" as a formal religion was a term not commonly used until many generations after Christ when a Roman emperor decided to use it for political purposes.

The name "Christian" was heard early in Antioch (Acts 11:19-30) but only as a respectful recognition that one group of believers were reflecting their close relationships with Jesus ("Christian" meaning family or friends of the Christ). The church soon went through a process of institutionalization that caused it to look much like the political set-up of the Roman Empire. At the top was the pope of Rome mirroring the emperor.

Despite this development, Jesus hadn't come to launch a new "religion" in competition with the many others. He came to announce the arriving of the kingdom of heaven that transcends all human categories and power arrangements and religious systems. The term "Christian" first appeared in broad public awareness as a powerful religious institution in a set of circumstances very different from those John knew when writing the Book of Revelation.

Persecution of the new faith had shifted to the rulers of the Empire using the faith to help retain power. A Roman politician in 315 A.D. decided that it was to his political advantage to adopt the Jesus movement of Judaism as his own. Many historians and theologians see in this secular decision the faith representing Jesus "falling" into serious compromise.

The Jesus people had become virtual wards of the state, strategic tools of the ruling empire. I'd now prefer not to be swept into just a little more of that fallenness. My name preference is also because much that is part of the "Christian" world today is not worth being associated with a serious believer in Jesus. It's better to be known simply as a dedicated disciple of Jesus than be painted with the broader "religious" brush.

Come Out from Among Them

Assuming the name "Christian" requires explaining what is meant, usually by adding adjectives like liberal, fundamentalist, ecumenical, pentecostal, Eastern, Western, Roman, Protestant, Evangelical, etc. Each of these wings of the faith has its own volatile history, sometimes not all very desirable.

Therefore, I prefer one's present faith identity to be tied more directly to the person of Jesus and less to the institutions and traditions that have gathered around that precious name. Such a shift relaxes the need to explain the "kind" of Christian one is. It's a modest attempt to distance oneself from the misdeeds of some past representatives of Christianity (the crusades, colonialism, the support for slavery, the persecution of Jews, and belittlement of women). I even hope for relief from being restricted by any given creedal tradition. Most if not all creeds have both strengths and inevitable frailties, value and limitations.

My concern is hardly new. I have traced a long trail of this reforming and re-branding impulse among Christians.[93] The Church of God movement (Anderson) has been saying since the late 1800s much of what I'm trying to affirm.[94] Denominations tend to be tribal and artificially narrowing of Christian fellowship and cooperation in mission. Formal and detailed creeds, especially when mandated for group membership, tend to stifle searching after the fuller truth. In the wrong hands they encourage a destructive division among believers.

Religious labels stereotype unfairly and isolate unnecessarily. I prefer breadth and wholeness. I hope to return to the freshness of the "apostolic" foundations of the faith. They are Jesus and his wisdom and power now mediated to us by the written Word and the ministry of his Spirit. I want to reach my hands to all believers without excessively honoring their human designations and affiliations that tend to be immediate roadblocks to Christian unity and mission.

This attempt to "come out" from the institutional divisions and "go back" to the apostolic basics may be too idealistic, of course. I like such idealism even if not quite reached. Granted, those who have sincerely tried to champion such idealism have experienced only partial success. Isn't that better than nothing?

I Admit to Being an Idealist

I admit to finding visionary idealism a good way to go in church life. It's at least a glimpse of what God intends for the church. The church is to be the fellowship of all "blood-washed" people who are committed to Jesus Christ and seized by a vision of all God's people functioning in fellowship and mission as one united and loving family of faith on mission in this world.

I don't want to be known as an adherent and advocate of some section of Christians who sit smugly in a corner and look critically at other believers who understand differently a point or two of doctrine or practice. I want to be identified with Jesus, with all his people, and with a reaching for the fullness of the truth that resides in the Master.

I want at least to try reaching beyond the common compromises of highly institutionalized churches and the tragically divided Christian world. Effective evangelism requires moving from fine talk about the church to an actual being the church in its intended holiness and unity.

Authority lies in the biblical revelation and not in any one body of believers and their current interpretations. Please call me a dedicated disciple of Jesus. The whole of the church belongs to me and I to it. The center of Christian faith is Jesus Christ, not any structure or creed or practice that has come to carry the name "Christian."

I want to keep moving beyond the common compromises and tragic divisions of our faith community. Christian history calls for considerable explanation to the public, and in some cases sincere apologies. Jesus himself needs no defense. His people and their actions often do.

One of my favorite books of Christian sermons recalls St. Partick saying, "I bind unto myself today the strong name of the Trinity."[95] Such binding is good enough for me!

****

Jesus with the Final Word

(in part a paraphrase of Luke-Acts)

The big question I posed to my disciples was, "Who am I?" I lived a life surrounded by major misunderstanding on almost every hand. Mary was shocked at her pregnancy, Joseph was quite confused, my disciples searched for answers, and the general public paraded a range of false impressions of me. Even those Jewish leaders who became convinced that I really was the expected "Messiah" badly misread what that meant. I wasn't the Messiah most hoped for, a military leader come to free the people with swords. I was a suffering servant of my Father come to save in quite another way.

The Romans hung me and over my head nailed, "Jesus of Nazareth, King of the Jews." Had I been a prophet, politician, rebel, insurrectionist, new King David, a threat to the Roman emperor? Yes and no, depending on how things get defined. The four New Testament Gospels tell the story well so that the truth of my identity eventually could emerge. Who are you who claim to be my people?

Are you church members following all the rules, odd people with heightened religious sensitivities, people trying to take over your culture and force all people to live according to my way of being? You are to be witnesses of me to the ends of the earth (Acts 1:8). Do you know what you are supposed to be telling people? Are you treating all persons with respect? If I came again as a helpless baby, would you also not believe and soon call for my death?

How do you want to be identified by today's public? Dare you be radically counter-cultural as I was? Will people misunderstand you? Are you ready for that? Luke's story of Christian beginnings

(Gospel of Luke and Book of Acts) traces my church from a virtual little sect of Judaism in Jerusalem to a universal expression of my Father seeking the whole world in love. That was possible because some people knew *who I really am* and they were prepared to be known as representing me at whatever the cost. Do you know me? Are you prepared? Try reading again Dr. Luke's material. He got it right. Follow me!

19

WHICH IS THE REAL CHURCH? NONE!

Beyond being a unique way of thinking, Christianity is intended to be a unique way of *linking*. The church binds together all the redeemed of God, living and dead. It's blessed with a measure of divinity and yet necessarily lives with much humanness. Each member is gifted by God to serve some need of the whole. Working together, the members are enabled to ensure the effectiveness of the church's life and mission.

How many "churches" are there? There are many Christian bodies going under different names and organized in various ways. Their beliefs range widely, at least in details, and their programming is anything but uniform. So which is the real church, the right one for you to join? There is no simple answer. One thing is clear. No church organization is the whole of the church and no religious body formed by humans is ever in itself the church of God.

The church is the gathering and the going of the people Jesus, a people caught in the middle. It's caught in time between being divinely birthed and humanly populated. It's also caught between yesterday, today, and tomorrow. It necessarily reaches back to Jesus himself and is nourished by all its saints and faith traditions of the past. Its commission is to cherish the past so that it may be a redeeming people in the settings of today. Meanwhile, it should be preparing itself to be the Bride anxious for the return of the Groom in some glorious tomorrow.

Apostolic, Catholic, Protestant

The biblical material concludes with a review of how a series of local congregations were doing in their lives and missions. The findings presented in the Book of Revelation are mostly discouraging. They were to be shining divine candlesticks when in fact they were lights struggling to stay burning or already having gone out. The church is a divine institution populated by immature pilgrim believers. It's always a people caught between heaven and earth.

After the bodily departure of Jesus from this world, there was a colony of heaven left behind to carry on his mission. This colony is the church, a divine beachhead, a beginning of God's tomorrow. It's indwelled by Christ's Spirit who conveys gifts to the members to make possible their special life and task. Our focus should be less on the humanness of church fellowships and their members and more on the power of God seeking to be at work in and through them.

A constant question arises. Because the church always has its human side, it's subject to the limitations of particular people and times. God always seeks to enable it to rise above its persistent limitations of understanding, maturity, and commitment. This is the "sanctifying" ministry from on high.

Meanwhile, believers link themselves together in various fellowships, each calling itself a "church," maybe even *the* church when overly arrogant. Which one of them should a believer join? The simple answer is, possibly any that's functioning well where you are as a sincere part of the whole church.

On that first Easter, attention began to shift away from the earthly Jesus. The community of his disciples celebrated the resurrection and soon were filled with the same life-giving Spirit. They were the new body of Jesus sharing significantly in his living, teaching, dying, and rising. The early church, despite all its limitations, was the community of believers in Jesus trying to be on its way to Christlikeness through the ongoing ministry of Christ's Spirit. The church is the instrument of Christ called to carry on his mission in the power of his Spirit.

Over the centuries the church often has strayed from its ideal nature and purpose. There are three necessities if the church is being true self, today's body of Christ. It must have a continuity with the past, especially with the decisive period recorded in the New Testament, thus being *apostolic*. It must have a willingness to profit from the whole of the Christian tradition, not just the isolated part that it happens to be, thus be *catholic*. Finally, it must have the courage to critique, adapt, and act in the present as God may command, thus be *protestant*. It always must protest any emerging deviations from its true self. The church can bless the world only if she is faithfully all three.[96]

Learn to Think Whole

There are many diverse appearances of the church and yet it's intended to be one. It may be in many places and have many members, functions, styles, and organizational patterns, but it cannot be the church if multiple bodies of Christ (Rom 12: 4-8; 1 Cor 12:30). Christians have been called into *one* body (Col 3:15) and are intended to be members together in that body (Eph 5: 30). We Jesus believers are to be members one of another (Eph 4:25).

Unfortunately, many Christians think of themselves primarily as members of a particular "church" (denomination). This affiliation too often goes to the extent of dulling awareness of the larger reality of the one body of Christ wherein true membership must lie. Belonging to a particular segment of the whole church is inevitable and acceptable under the right conditions. What is unacceptable is belonging to any segment that fails to encourage a vision of the wholeness of the one church and fails to function with the understanding that it is not itself the whole.

All Christian traditions and congregations should downplay any primary and exclusive self-identification. Such include a particular church leader (Mennonite, Baptist, Wesleyan), church government (Presbyterian), church headquarters (Rome, Church of God--Anderson or Cleveland), doctrinal distinctive (Pentecostal), spiritual phenomenon (Quaker), idealistic state (Reformed), national affiliation (Church of England), or ministry function (Salvation Army).[97]

Instead, all Christian fellowship groups should identify themselves as closely as possible with the one church envisioned by the New Testament. Particular traditions of the church may carry emphases needed by the whole body, gifts they have for all those in

Christ. The concern comes when such emphases that should be gifts for the good of the whole are allowed to function as walls dividing from the whole. As Christians, our primary identity is to be those *in Christ,* members among all of God's people whatever the local affiliation.

One Christian university has advertised itself with the proper balance of denominational roots and an all-church vision. It called itself "Historically Orthodox, clearly Evangelical, genuinely Ecumenical, and distinctively Wesleyan." Here's an appreciative sense of the entire Christian tradition, a desire to be catholic (ecumenical) with recognition of a particular Christian tradition, the Wesleyan, that is highlighted for the sake of carrying particular truths for the good of the whole Christian heritage.[98] We are one in our diversity and are to be better because of the diversity.

Dynamic and Stabilizing

There can be no avoiding the basic paradox of church membership. By virtue of our birthright as converted children of God, we are members of the whole church. By virtue of personal, family, geographic, and historical circumstances, we also find our places to function in the life of the church by becoming associated with a particular historical expression of its life. We belong at one time to the whole and to part of the whole.

Here's the paradox. The whole without concrete and localized expressions of itself is little more than a dream. But concrete and local expressions of the church must be defined by an intentional orientation to the whole or they become alien strains hurtful to the whole. We members are caught between the whole and being part of the whole. If any voluntary association of Christians builds artificial and unnecessary walls between Christians, that association ceases to be a legitimate part of the whole.

There are two essential dimensions to church life, the *dynamic* (charismatic) and the *stabilizing* (institutional). One creates and enriches church life and the other seeks to order that life for its mission and needed accountability. These twin dimensions can come into conflict. While stabilizing is necessary, its forms and officers and programs are only temporary vehicles for the life and work of the Spirit of God. God also gives spiritual gifts and brings new life, insight, and passion--the *dynamic*. Church members then seek to remember the faith correctly, enrich the church with their gifting, and discipline community life for the sake of Christ's mission in the world—the *stabilizing*.

The church is the called people "who know themselves to be standing together in relationship to the God who saves them. It's the fellowship in which disciples teach and support each other. It's the holy assembly of those who live and serve in righteousness by the grace of God and through the presence and power of God's Spirit. It's the people called together to reflect the loving and reaching divine image to the world."[99] Whatever Christian group is joined, a believer should be sure that he or she in this one church!

****

Jesus with the Final Word

(in part a paraphrase of Luke 7:36-8:3)

No human fellowship of believers is the real church just because of the name over the door or the creed repeated constantly. It comes down to how people are seen and treated and how my Father is honored. You are to worship in Spirit and truth. I am the truth and it is my Spirit who forms and inflames the church's life. You are to open the church doors, not close them on people who are the most vulnerable or least like you.

Here are two big tasks as my followers. Build bridges and tear down walls. Be the gracious host who rejoices in anyone who is kind to me and hoping for a new beginning in life. Never forget that woman who was abused. She had an evil reputation and came into a home where I was the guest. She was especially kind to me and upset my Pharisee host greatly. He belittled her, saying that if I was who I claimed to be, I would have had nothing to do with her (Lk 7:36-50). He was so wrong. My church must be so right.

The real sin is the ugly bias that divides the world into sinners and saints and assumes that my Father honors the divide. Humans tend to isolate and conquer "sinners" as they choose. In fact, while all people are sinners, by the power of forgiving love all can be restored and become saints of my Holy Father. Anyone may become an honored church member who comes asking humbly in faith. Act as welcoming and healing agents of mine and thus together be the real church!

20

WHO'S IN AND WHO'S OUT? DEPENDS!

We humans are tribal, usually making clear who belongs with us and who doesn't. Must the church of Jesus be another exclusive club where we set restrictive membership rules based on personal or group understandings and preferences? Could Jesus get into your church's membership? Is safeguarding the church's boundaries supposed to be the preoccupation of believers?

Deciding who's "in" or "out" is a big issue that has troubled the church of all times. Isn't that God's business? True members are those born again by the blood of the Lamb. We tend to go further, insisting that the new babes in Christ conform to our local definitions of what is proper believing and behavior, sometimes both defined in considerable detail. Where do we draw the line? Who decides? How thick should the line be?

Since God hopes to save all persons, the divine intention is for the church of Jesus to be an "inclusive" community. The problem is determining exactly who is included in the "inclusive." The church is for all, reaching to all, loving all, and yet distinctive, not championing just anything. It's to be the community of new-creation persons, a community of the "converted" seeking to reflect the life of God in their own lives.

Through the doors of the church is invited all manner of fallen humanity. They are offered the hope of being community members of the new humanity in Christ. But to what degree must they conform to what we look like and how we think and act in this church?

Who Can Be Members?

An acceptable expectation is that new members at least not remain who they once were. Now anxious for Jesus to be the center of their existence, they are to be willing to conform to Christ-likeness. Jesus embarrassed and angered the ultra-conservative Jewish leaders of his day by forgiving some of the least respected people he encountered—Roman soldiers, lepers, moral degenerates, and women, even a Samaritan woman. He expected change without always detailing it in advance.

Who can be in and who must stay out was a huge issue in the earliest Christian church. Paul, at first a Jewish killer of Christians, soon was spearheading the Jesus community and taking a stance daring indeed for a Jew. He began insisting that the new faith community of Jesus is not to be merely another Jewish sect. Jesus was much more that an extra-special Jew.

Gentiles (people outside the Jewish community) were now said to be candidates for church membership if they accepted Jesus as Lord, and that *without first becoming Jewish.* The good news from God is that the message of redemption and new life is not for Jews alone and any others willing to adopt the identity and trappings of Judaism. It's for all people who become God's children regardless of their cultural and religious backgrounds, and without first conforming to a given set of religious traditions and practices.

This opening wide the doors of God's people was very controversial and still is. As can be seen simmering in the New Testament, alarming many Jewish leaders and even some Jewish Christians. Paul paid a heavy price for going against the prevailing view that God had chosen a special people, the Jews, and definitely not all the outsiders. One extreme rabbi was saying that God created Gentiles only to stoke the fires of hell! Surely God would not honor a new believer in Jesus unless that person first converted to Judaism.

The evangelistic dynamite that exploded into the sudden expansion of the early Christian church was that salvation isn't dependent on who people were ethnically or racially or what they had done before. It's dependent solely on what God in Jesus *had done for them* and then their response to that undeserved divine grace. Membership in the true church of Jesus is based on one thing only. It's a willing receiving of new life in the Spirit of Christ. It's not based on any tribalistic heritage or religious label or good deed.

The "Conjunctive" Church

Christians over the centuries often have gone much too far in their church tribalisms. This includes persecuting Jews and ignoring most of the "Old" Testament as wholly outdated, beneath the Jesus standard, hardly necessary for Christians. This false move must be countered strongly. It's not Jesus-like, not nearly as "inclusive" as it ought to be.[100] To not know and appreciate the "Old" is to make the "New" Testament very difficult to understand. To arrive at a drama only at intermission is to make the final scenes of its unfolding plot confusing at best.

A strength of John Wesley's theology is its *both/and* character. He affirms both God's sovereignty and human freedom, salvation by faith and the necessity of resulting good works, the continuing value of the Law despite the clear priority of God's grace. John was both rational and poetic, right-brained and left-brained. He lived at the height of the Age of Reason and at the beginning of the new interest in human experience, emotion, and relations. He was sensitive to the Eastern and Western traditions of Christianity.

This "conjunctive" nature of Christian theology runs deep. Parallel truths remain joined. God's truth transcends our rational tools and categories. It's fundamentally reasonable, even while being profoundly personal. Christian theological dialogue must include many voices, past and present, global and local, West and East, moving across cultures in an ongoing engagement of biblical teaching and contextual challenges. This openness to a breadth of essential inclusions is crucial to the fullness and evangelistic effectiveness of Christian understanding and mission.

Life in Jesus Christ is a grateful response to God's love. It brings an inclusive freedom in Christ, although never an uncontrolled allowing of any moral license. The new life is superintended by the Spirit of Jesus, kept in line by the standards and mission of Jesus. The scandal is that God has opened the door to all people, most being unlike us in many ways. We tend to resist, preferring to choose our spiritual brothers and sisters according to our private human standards. Doing so is Christianity gone wrong. It's the dark back alley of sinful exclusiveness.

A common saying carries much weight and many questions. We Christians are to be *in* the world but not *of* it. We are to share the good news of Jesus everywhere, with everyone, believing that it is for all. Meanwhile, we are to be different from the world. We are "resident aliens," distinct with special standards, clear boundaries, ways that make clear that "we" are not "they," even if we have good news *for all*. This is difficult territory to traverse!

The challenge is defining the *exclusive* boundaries without violating the *inclusive* message. As human cultures shift, defining keeps being a fresh challenge. We must go back to Jesus who was not seeking to destroy his Jewish identity or its Law and yet was bringing an overarching law of love that signaled a very new day for his people and for all people.

One Christian reform movement features the slogan "We Reach Our Hands in Fellowship to Every Bloodwashed One." This included the meaning "regardless of their denominational affiliation." All in Christ are to be considered one with all believers, their diversity notwithstanding. However, what about those believers who are different from us in ways other than religious affiliation, such as in doctrinal beliefs or cultural practices or ethnic and sexual identities? Such a question keeps driving us back to Jesus in search of the biblical boundaries of inclusiveness.[101]

Secure Only *in Christ*

This much is clear. All persons are truly loved as God's children and welcome to participate in the church's fellowship as believers, new creations in the making. When it comes to church leadership, stricter limits may prevail (1 Tim 3:1-7, etc.). Ministerial ordination may be judged out of the question for some believers who yet lack the basics of the new creation as understood by the ordaining body. Reaching to all blood-washed ones is a sincere vision that can have elements of exclusion in the midst of its inclusiveness. One may be loved and belong without being chosen to represent the church body as an especially matured and model member.

The unity generated by inclusion is the general intent. Its boundaries are set only by what is understood to be anything biblically mandated as beyond acceptability. We hear the Master's loving voice saying, "You are loved, forgiven, made acceptable in my Father's sight. Now go and sin no more." In this we hear a radical inclusion and an implied exclusion. The followers of Jesus are to be different, Jesus-like, on a new life path. Once matured in that new life, they then qualify to represent the church as one of its recognized leaders.

Is a believer who once gets in the church guaranteed to always be in? The phrase "eternal security" often is used to claim an assured completing of the faith journey once a start is made on the Christian way. How do we gain security that never ends? By never turning back! We are secure only while *in Christ*. We remain in Christ by abiding faith and faithfulness.

Who's in and who's out? It depends not on who you are and where you come from but on what you choose to be and do. Christians choose to live under the gracious reign of God but always retain the ability to reverse that choice. We reap the reward offered only if we endure. If we do, full assurance is definite.

> Under His wings I am safely abiding,
> though the night deepens and the tempest is wild.
> Still I can trust Him, I know He will keep me;
> He has redeemed me, and I am his child.[102]

****

Jesus with the Final Word

(in part a paraphrase of Luke 13:1-9)

To be my disciples and members of my church, you must have a real change of mind that results in fruit-bearing. Let me be clear. It's an entirely new life, a lifetime quest, the journey from a fallen lostness to a restored holiness. Come to me and be fed. Drink of the cup and eat of the bread of life. The word *metanoia* means to repent and really change your mind and life. This is more than an intellectual shift of thinking. It's changing the focus of your whole life, a change of your way of being and living.

To really be "converted" is to live in a distinctly different way, my way. My disciple Luke points to the full ramifications of repentance. "Turn to God and do deeds consistent with repentance" (Acts 26:20). When you call other people to repent, never focus only on the forgiveness of past sin. The call should include commitment to bearing future fruit worthy of repentance. Doing this is to be one of mine, members of my church.

New disciples and church members are to have their eyes open to see human need and their hearts open to serve this need. To bear such fruit is the natural result of feeding on the richness of myself, the Bread of Life. There's little worth in an apple tree that consistently fails to produce apples. My Father is a patient and compassionate gardener. Church membership is costly. It involves a real changing of the mind and a definite activation of life in the direction consistent with that change.

21

WHY READ THE BIBLE? DON'T!

The Bible is a means, not a goal. Don't read and then try to *use* it for your personal agendas. That's done much too often. Read it with the church and in light of the risen Christ, and then let it shape you into the image of Christ. That's the Bible's goal, allowing it *to read you*!

A wrong reading can be worse than no reading at all. You can read and then can claim that your personal preferences are also the demands of God—and you've found a verse or two to prove it. Of course every believer should read. To be exposed to the written Word can be life itself. It's just that it helps so much if the Bible is read properly.

It's worth saying again. Don't read the Bible. Well, at least read it carefully, not alone if possible and certainly not to support your preferred understandings and agendas. It's best read in light of the wisdom of the church across the ages. Especially determine to do this. Let the Bible *read you!*

Objectivity and Subjectivity

The Bible is God's intended means to a very important end. That end isn't to satisfy the reader's curiosities or answer all personal questions. It's to transform the reader into the image of Jesus Christ whose Spirit originally inspired the Bible for that very purpose.

Objectivity may be a good thing, but trying to achieve it is never free of some subjectivity for us humans. If you think otherwise, you're deluded. I've authored five biographies, each of significant and very different people.[103] There is a commonality within each of these works. Since I'm the one who researched and wrote them, my way of understanding these persons and telling their stories is always subtly present. This adds a level of subjectivity to what I tried to be very objective and fair reporting of another's life story.

I told these stories as the facts dictated, being as accurate as possible while realizing that I could never know all the facts. The human factor always remains. The stories have been put in contexts of my creation and expressed in my style and language and range of knowing and not knowing about the subject. I've worked hard to keep to a minimum the downsides of this subjectivity. Each of these stories I've called *a* biography and not *the* biography. Another biographer almost certainly would write the same life story a bit differently.

What about the life story of Jesus? The four New Testament "Gospels" aren't quite formal biographies, but they head in that direction. Each is about the same amazing person, each telling his story in a somewhat different way. Christians are convinced that all four are divinely *inspired*, entrusted to us by God's Spirit, each dependable in its distinctive way.

This divine inspiring obviously hasn't eliminated each author's individual slant, particular intended audience, and available sources of information and manner of expression. No matter. The Spirit hovered over them all. Each is dependable while the fuller sufficiency is found in the four taken together.

Don't Find What's Not There

I recall a New Testament scholar announcing this. "How exciting that the four New Testament tellers of the Jesus story sometimes report the same incident with differing and even conflicting details!" Why excitement over apparent confusion in the inspired biblical text? He said the presence of minor confusions, and they are few and very minor, mean that each writer was so excited about the truth of what had happened that he told things breathlessly, not checking to see if all his details fit exactly with the detailed telling of others.

Slightly varying perceptions of the same truth only serve to authenticate the general truthfulness of each telling. What we have is a dependable biblical text, not one manipulated carefully by later editors to make it appear "inerrant." If a tiny variance of detail is ever noted, thank the Lord! They are real testimonies by humans of things beyond the human.

These Gospels are not free of all human elements, but that doesn't matter. The Spirit hovered over their preparation and now hovers over their being read, making them capable of achieving the intentions of divine revelation.[104] What God has provided is wholly sufficient for the divine intention. We are to know Jesus as God with us. We are to be changed into his likeness.

There should be no fixation with the supposed "inerrancy" of the text. Focus should be on the Spirit's working through the text to lead us to Jesus Christ, the fully trustworthy revelation of God. Fussing about inconsequential variances in the text is a modern literary distraction from the text's intent. The Bible is pointing to the love and perfections and intentions of God and our possible life transformation because of them.

It's time for what has been called a "re-enchanting" of the biblical text.[105] We must become open to encountering God's actual presence as we study the text. Then should come a willingness to live from that experienced Mystery, the divinity behind and speaking through the sacred text. There is to be no worshipping of the words themselves.

Here's a fact very important for quality biblical understanding. If neither we nor the Gospel writers can keep all subjectivity from our writings, it's also true that none of us can separate ourselves from the subjectivity *of our reading*.

Present reading of anything, including the Bible, is like a mirror. We humans look down a deep well to see what's there. What we think we see often is our own faces reflecting off the water at the bottom. We tend to see what we already know, expect to see, and may have assumed all along. Our tendency is to place new information in the same old boxes where we already have previous information stored.

Matthew was a Jew committed to reversing the Jewish tendency of his time to see in their wells of Scripture reading a coming Messiah much like what they wanted to receive and were sure they needed. His Gospel is full of saying to such Jews that the story of

Jesus is indeed everywhere in their ancient writings *if only they had known how to read them properly*.

Following his resurrection, Jesus walked with two Jews on the road to Emmaus and freshly explained the Scriptures to them *in light of himself*. Mirrors shifted and the same biblical words began reporting new meanings to these men. The Scriptural words hadn't changed, just the human understandings of their meaning.

The fuller truth about Jesus is available only in the blending of the four New Testament Gospel accounts, each supplementing the others. In fact, the biblical view of many subjects requires the balancing of different emphases of a given subject found in different parts of the Bible. When dare not insist that a single phrase or sentence found in one biblical spot is necessarily the whole of a matter. How easy it is to violate biblical revelation and lie with a little piece of the truth! Better not to read than read in a fragmented way that yields false results.

Learn Spirit Bible Reading

The Bible is intended to be a *transparency* of the Divine more than an encyclopedia of religious information. The Bible is less what we think we can see *in it* and more what we are helped by God to see *through it*. If God had wanted to communicate with scientific precision, "God would have used the language of mathematics, the only truly precise language we have. But, of course, you can't say 'I love you' in algebra."[106]

The Bible enables us to see the Spirit of God present and at work. The Spirit assists us to see the Father acting in the Son, to see beyond sin and death to present and future resurrection life, and also beyond today's suffering to coming eternal blessedness. The Spirit helps us move beyond our unanswered questions to the God of redeeming love in whom resides all answers not yet available to us.

Our claims to "what the Bible teaches" must remain cautiously open to the larger wisdom of the ongoing teaching ministry of God's interpreting Spirit. Responsible Bible reading is at the heart of the church's life. Irresponsible Bible reading haunts the church with blindness and division. We should read to encounter *God in Jesus* as understood through the Spirit. This is done best in the midst of the reading and believing community. The church should be a fellowship of ongoing conversation about what the Spirit is saying to God's people about the inspired treasure found within the Bible.

Bible readers never should be satisfied with finding a few religious "facts" and memorizing a few favorite quotes. These tend to get put into artificial boxes and forced unfairly on other believers. We are to allow God to shape us into new persons who are anxious to read through the Spirit's eyes and learn from fellow believers. Of supreme importance is allowing the biblical text to focus its attention *on us*, our blindness, our sin, and our hope in Christ.

Again, the reading goal isn't to provide answers to all our spiritual and ethical questions. It's to guide and enable a *reshaping of us*, the readers, into the image of God known best in Jesus. We are to go to the biblical text realizing that it intends to *come to us*, and not necessarily as we might expect. We are to read in order to *be read* and changed into the image of Jesus for the sake of the world.

The biblical words are divine *means,* not in themselves the divine goal. God's inspiring intent is not that we disciples become voracious readers and doctrinal experts. It's rather that we become Christ-like persons. Jesus promised that, as his Spirit originally inspired the writers to record sufficiently the story of God with us in Jesus, the same Spirit now will inspire us new readers to understand the ancient lines properly for ourselves and our times.

If you insist on not reading this way, maybe it's best that you not read at all! To *use* the Bible is likely to *abuse* it. Allow God to find and change you by means of the reading and the reward will be great indeed.

> Come, Holy Spirit. Focus our reading on your living presence and change us into the image of Jesus! Help us *use* but not *abuse* the biblical text. Back to the blessed old Bible, yes, but *with integrity*!

****

Jesus with the Final Word

(in part a paraphrase of John 12:1-8)

Read the revealed Scripture, my friends, and remember God's great actions of yesterday. However, don't allow your looking back to block your openness to seeing my Father acting in fresh and amazing ways today! Yesterday has wisdom to share, especially about me. Even so, this wisdom can sour into meaninglessness if you get stuck back there and lose my Spirit's connection with today's fresh possibilities.

Going back in grateful memory is a necessary resource for going forward. The Bible is a book of remembering and anticipating. The biblical purpose is always bringing change and going on. My Spirit's ministry is to help you read properly, especially to know me and my ways on your behalf.

Focus not on yesterday's death but on tomorrow's resurrection. Determine to look ahead and be part of what my Father's now intending to do in and through you. I'm no longer on the cross. Dance with joy around my empty grave. Ask not, "How has it always to be done?" I much prefer another question. "What are our next steps together, Lord?" Be open to a new thing. Don't be paralyzed by what death once did to me or can do to you. I am the eternal life that overcomes the old and brings forth the new!

22

READ THE WHOLE BIBLE? NO!

The last essay focused on the importance of reading the Bible properly. Now we think about how much of it is to be read. Read all the Bible if you can, of course, but this is a huge challenge and most people will fail in the attempt. The Bible is a lengthy and very diverse library. Short attention spans coupled with the many other problems discourage most people.

The important thing is to hear well all the Bible's big messages meant for you. There is a way to do this successfully without reading endlessly. Even though some might disagree on what the Bible intends as central and critical, a consensus has been reached by numerous Bible scholars. It's better to hit the highpoints than get lost in a sea of weeds.

The previous essay made clear *why* believers should read the Bible. We ourselves are to be read by the Spirit and changed into the image of Jesus. The Bible's primary purpose is *formational*, not *informational*. It was inspired less to answer our questions and more to meet our deepest needs. Christians believe that the Bible reflects God's will and ways. The big questions are about what divine ways and what human needs.

Not the Easiest to Read

The actual Bible reading of most Christians today falls far short of any ideal. A comprehensive coverage of the huge text is rarely done. The problem is more than busy schedules and short attention spans. Even serious disciples get lost and confused in the mass of biblical detail and in the face of the many unknowns of ancient places, cultures, practices, and names. There are whole chapters in the Old

Testament that seem gross, unethical, so unlike Jesus, difficult to understand, even hard on the stomach.[107]

The circumstance of very limited Bible reading by the average believer should say something to planners of Sunday worship. A frequent reading of the Bible in such public settings is very important. Many and probably most believers today read very little of the Bible between worship services, even if numerous copies are found around their homes. Sermons and other elements of public worship need substantial Bible content. Otherwise, many of the members will quietly starve spiritually from lack of exposure to the sacred text.

The Bible is comprised of sixty-six separate "books" involving some 1,200 chapters as typically edited and captioned in modern translations. This mass of biblical material isn't arranged chronologically or often even by themes. Some of it goes into great detail about matters now completely outdated. Stories get repeated by different writers, occasionally with different slants, even with a little contrasting information.

If God were to have written this book for us without human involvement, surely it would be a more readable product. The style would be more consistent and, at least for haughty Americans, all in English and not ancient Hebrew and Greek that even the best scholars struggle to translate in agreement with each other.

A little book like Esther doesn't seem to belong at all. It's about ancient political intrigue with no mention of God. The last book in the biblical collection is mostly an "apocalyptic" presentation that urgently requires special literary coaching before reading. It looks on the surface like a Jurassic Park movie designed to frighten and defy contemporary understanding and maybe stimulate teenage imaginations.

Since there's no way to be a mature Christian while remaining biblically illiterate, there needs to be a way around these reading obstacles. We're not all going to complete a Bible major in college, and for some graduates I know even that wasn't very successful. What then? Should every biblical word be read, maybe every year by every believer? That would be fine, but hardly necessary, and for most believers impractical.

A Reading Plan

The important point isn't speed and volume of Bible reading so much as depth of hearing the divine voice that leads to depth understanding and obedience. The Spirit of God comes to the reader through the written Word. While in seminary, I took a class in second-year Greek. The professor chose the Gospel of John to probe closely in its linguistic original. After one full semester, we had not reached chapter two! We had mined every possible theological nuance supposedly buried in the ancient syntax and nearly lost in ancient word meanings. We heard the professor if not the Spirit.

When people step into the library of the Bible's extensive contents, often they get lost among its many shelves, twisting aisles, cultural categories, literary styles, and alternate languages. Readers need skilled librarians to get around, commentaries to help interpret what's found, dictionaries to define words never heard before, and historians to explain ancient settings basic to the backgrounds of the biblical text. Very few church members will manage this well.

There's a helpful plan for extensive Bible exposure that doesn't stress the need to try dealing with everything in the whole of the biblical text. It's organized around the Christian Year and honors the intent of the whole Bible in the process. The focus is on highlights of Scripture encountered in the contexts of the annual seasons of a Christian faith year, the life of Jesus, and dimensions of needed spiritual growth. It allows a reader to see the big picture as biblically intended. It inclines the reader toward personal impact and spiritual change more than private textual selections and broad-scale frustration.[108]

This proposed reading plan is less disjointed than trying to go from Genesis to Revelation. There are fewer temptations to focus on stray details or isolated verses while being totally mystified by many others. Key life themes faced in biblical yesterdays are brought forward for the facing of Christian life today. There is constant encouragement to listen to God's Spirit who is eager to interpret and apply enduring truths in changed times and places.

When finished with this approach to a year-long journey through the Bible, will every biblical word have been read? No, but that doesn't really matter. The whole of the Bible will have been read in a truly biblical way. Encountered will have been the pivotal texts, the central biblical truths, with everything faced that God wants known and done today. Sung will have been praise to God with Jews and Christians. Psalms and hymns often appear because they address every season and circumstance of the believer's spiritual journey.

One Bible scholar organized the many psalms into three groups, Orientation, Disorientation, and Reorientation.[109] The first presents the things of life and faith as they should be and originally were when God created. The second recognizes that things have gone seriously wrong and samples the pain. Even when confusion and suffering are at their most intense, there arrives the third group. These celebrate the grace and guidance of God who suddenly sets bleeding feet and broken hearts on ground higher than known before. One need not necessarily read all the psalms. A few from each group will accomplish the critical task.

In a similar manner, following the Christian Year provides focus on the many dimensions of needed spiritual formation. It's especially sensitive to life themes and their current social challenges. Presented is a roadmap through the whole of Scripture that speaks to each phase of the typical Christian's faith journey, illumined in part by the journeys of many who went this way long ago.

Annual Listening to the Spirit

Traveling these biblical ancient paths will help believers in their understandings and spiritual advances. Readers who employ the spiritual art of listening to the Spirit across a year and obeying will be changed into the image of Jesus Christ. The genius of God's Word, beyond recording the critical past of Jewish and Christian faith, is that it serves as a medium through which God still speaks freshly to willing hearts.

Today's Christians who spend only an hour or two a week with this plan will be everywhere they need to be in the Bible in twelve months. Spending another hour or two each week in serious prayer about the Spirit's biblical speaking for that week will allow encounters with the biblical text to impact the depths of life's cleansing and growth needs.

Using the format of the Christian Year provides fifty-two opportunities to focus on selected portions of Scripture, usually each week two from each Testament. Each portion might be a verse or chapter that presents a key biblical message from God. Each is reviewed in an all-Bible perspective with its contemporary challenge to the reader's spiritual growth and service. Any part of the Bible is to be understood in light of the entire biblical revelation.

No biblical book is ignored and no spiritual growth need neglected. Nothing ancient is left unexplained, no difficult language left confusing. Granted, following this plan won't make the reader a master theologian or admired historian of ancient times. No matter. The important point is this. God wants the reader to be encountered by the central biblical texts in their fullness of intent for the living of these days.

We long for the day envisioned by the prophet Jeremiah when people will really *know* God (Jer 31:34). The word "know" here means more than gaining knowledge *about*. It means acquiring knowledge *of* by way of personal experience *with*. We are to read the Bible to be *changed* as much or more than to be *informed*. While we can't all be Bible scholars, we all can and should be exposed to core biblical messages that lead to Christ-like new life and Spirit-inspired world mission.

****

Jesus with the Final Word

(in part a paraphrase of John 1:1-5 and Hebrews 1:1-3)

As I care for my sheep, you also are to be caring for the sheep I have in many folds. Am I the Messiah? The convincing is in the doing. Don't try to put on impressive displays of divine showmanship. Be humble and loving, giving fully of yourself and yielding to others in love. Don't assume that reading every page of the Bible has some special value for your spiritual life. It's reading in depth that makes the difference, learning the major spiritual themes stressed throughout, seeing the truths that I now have or soon will fulfill. The mass of biblical detail is relatively unimportant, especially if it distracts you from relating ever more intimately to me through my Spirit.

The church must not hinder today's moving of God by its obsession with what has been before. You must be open to recognizing and celebrating what yet can be by the power of my Spirit. Read the Bible as much as you can and spend some time walking with me as I did with those men on their way to Emmaus. They read the Word but hardly understood what it meant. That's why I walked with them and opened their eyes. Are you reading with your eyes closed?

Cultural expressions, theological explorations, and worship practices are widely diverse in my church. People who are equally faithful in following me don't always look and act exactly alike or even read the Bible in the same way. Even so, there remains only one message. In the midst of potentially distracting diversities, focus on the unifying message of my Father's revelation. Read the Word, find in it the ultimate Word, myself, and become agents of that Word in your time.

23

WHICH CHURCH MUSIC? DIVERSE!

The church often struggles with its personalities, programs, organizations, and worship styles. None are ultimate, none the best in all times and places. Diversity can be enriching and disturbing. Church health depends on embracing the diversity, balancing with care the "classic" and "contemporary" in light of the times and crowd at hand.

Christian ears and souls are tuned differently. The great organs of the European cathedrals are one musical expression of Christian faith in "high" worship. Another that's "low" is the nineteenth-century holiness people borrowing songs from bar rooms and street singers as the chosen medium for successfully conveying the Christian message to very different folks. High and low doesn't imply better or worse, just more relevant.

A stern Scottish church leader once went to London, so the story goes. During a Sunday walk in Hyde Park he spotted what he judged a revolting scene. Members of the royal family were riding horses for pleasure on the Sabbath day! He complained openly about this obvious violation of the Lord's Day by the detested English hierarchy. One young pastor heard and countered with this.

"But even our Lord and his disciples walked through the cornfields on the Sabbath and plucked whatever grain their bodies needed."

"Aye," shot back the elder man, "that may have been true. But two wrongs donna make a right!" Apparently, when a mind is made up, mere logic doesn't make a difference, even about an action approved by Jesus himself.

Balancing the Halves

What is necessary in Christian worship is a careful balancing of the two halves of one truth. Recently the focus has been on "praise songs," worship teams, and the ear-pounding of drums. Worship health calls for a rich diversity. Jesus spoke of proper worship being conducted "in spirit and in truth" (Jn 4:24). This fullness of focus can be thought of as personal experience and relationship change (*spirit*) that is consciously rooted in essential theology (*truth*).

A fresh emphasis now appears needed to secure the truth side of this worship paradox. We dare not raise a generation of "praise junkies" who lean too far toward individualism, personal spiritual experience, and emotional release and excitement, all good except when one-sided. Here's the justification for the current emphasis. "How else do we satisfy the worship needs of today's 'postmodern' people? They want intimacy, immediacy, and intense experiences and relationships." Shouldn't we give people what they want and need?

Yes—and no. Any significant over-emphasis on individualistic praise designed to foster an experiencing of the immediate presence of God risks serious negative impact over time. It's the loss of the necessary theological substance that must be the foundation of all authentic Christian "experience." Feeling the faith is good. So is knowing what is to be felt and for what purpose.

The either/or approach to a complex situation is rarely helpful. The many "spiritual songs" that celebrate experiencing the faith are appropriate and yet must be accompanied by the theologically rich framework of classic hymns. Today's secular environment has infused the Christian community with a preference for volume, emotion, beat, innovation, and individualism.

When on their own, these elements of worship risk neglecting other essential things, like thoughtful and God-centered congregational participation with deep theological understanding. We now often see the majority of a congregation standing, clapping to the music, feeling strongly while thinking shallowly at best about Christian theological substance.

Worshippers often watch as a musically skilled group, "on stage" and carefully rehearsed, is being featured. The group stands in spotlights further creating a "performance" atmosphere. Meanwhile, the average congregational member is losing the ability to read music and blend voices in the beauty of "parts" singing. More importantly, what's happening unintentionally is a relative loss of being in real touch with the basics of biblical Christianity.

Great Truths Are Paradoxical

Much Christian music is theologically rich and has proven "relevant" regardless of shifting human cultures. There must be congregational worship participation with mind and heart, bowed knees and engaged minds, the reading of the Bible and the singing of the soul. This multi-sided need not include any extreme criticism of "contemporary worship." Its many merits include freedom in Christ, joyous spiritual "experiences," and the use of current language relevant to the contemporary culture.

The point is the need to retain the paradox. In the process of celebrating Christian experience, we must not leave behind a new generation that lacks knowledge of the theological foundations of the Christian faith. Biblical illiteracy already is at an alarming level in society and increasingly even in the church. Theological illiteracy is now adding to the dangerous vacuum.

Friends and I recently put together a major two-volume biblical devotion guide designed to highlight the needed theological balancing. It's titled *A Year with Rabbi Jesus* and insists that theater must never overwhelm theology. Here is substance mixed with song and prayer, *spirit* linked directly to *truth*. Now there also is the companion book *Golden Nuggets* presenting the best of Christian theological thinking in small chunks understandable by anyone and workable into any balanced worship plan.[110]

The great truths of Christian faith are themselves paradoxical. God is three in one, Jesus truly human and truly God with us. The Bible is a divinely inspired human production. Another pivotal reality is that the worship of the Christian community must honor the full range of the substance-style paradox. There is a range of musical types that are endorsed and all encouraged for healthy Christian congregations.

The three types (styles) of music are to worship "with gratitude in your hearts, sing psalms, hymns, and spiritual songs" (Col 3:16). Simple definitions of these three are:

--**Hymns** are carefully crafted musical confessions about the nature and work of God;[111]
--**Psalms** are memories of the ways of God in the many circumstances of life;
--**Spiritual** *songs* are current celebrations of our direct experiences of God with us.

These three are the products of the faith's theologians, poets, and witnesses, with the differing emphases of mind, memory, and emotion. Christian worship needs them all.

The first is foundational and must be biblically grounded and thoughtfully stated. The others are increasingly devotional and emotionally expressive of experiences with this divine foundation. Without the grounding, worship easily becomes misguided and self-serving. Without the relational richness of the second and third types, worship tends to become impersonal and abstract, lacking the joyous wisdom and engaging the immediacy of the believer in worship with God presently and obviously active.

A healthy Christian congregation needs the songs of the Bible, the songs of the ages, and the songs of the moment. It needs songs that express the soul, stretch the mind, and rejoice the heart. It needs hymnbooks and chorus songs. Believers need to stand and clap in excitement and also kneel and pray in silence. Faith always must be personal but never individualistic. Worship is to be a community of faith praising God together for who God is and what God has done and now is doing for us in Christ.

Worship always should include sections of thoughtful theological instruction and affirmation. These are God-centered, calling our attention upward with a lofty message that draws believers beyond the immediate, the individual, and the earthly. They seek to connect us with God by our listening to divine revelation and being encouraged to respond appropriately. This brings us back to Bible hearing as well as voices singing.

Worship a Rehearsal for Heaven

Our current time is one of dramatic social shifts and global threats of unimaginable proportions. Membership in believing communities of rich fellowship is more critical than ever. Various non-Christian religious communities are teaching self-help philosophies as means of gaining inner peace, often with no reference to the existence of a transcendent God from whom all blessings flow. "Spirituality" has become a common public interest, although often far distanced from any rootage in biblical revelation.

What does Christian worship need to be especially in this environment? Spiritual songs of testimony are clearly needed, although never separated from the sturdy grounding of the great hymns of the faith. Let's sing our hearts out in hymn affirmations of truths that transcend the shifting winds of public opinion and passing time.

For present guidance, historic examples, and direct biblical support of full-orbed Christian worship adequate for this day, all developed around seasonal themes for each Sunday of the Church Year, consult the two volumes of *A Year with Rabbi Jesus*.[112] The editors have included biblical devotionals, each musically enriched, and theologically supported. They base the work on this wisdom:

> May we study the Word of God and learn of God's identity and gracious activity by singing again those great truths that secure the necessary theological base of our immediate experiences of God's wonderful Spirit. We sing together on earth to give praise to God in heaven. We are lifted on eagle wings of love to the joy of the communion of saints. The worship we do here on earth is merely a rehearsal for what we will do eternally in heaven.

****

Jesus with the Final Word

(in part a paraphrase of Psalm 98, John 4:24, and Col 3:16)

My dear disciples, know that my Father is beyond your sight, information, and even imagination, and yet so close by your side. The big theological words are *transcendent* and *imminent*. The first emphasizes the *so-beyond-us* reality of my Father. The second points to his *so-nearness*, nearer than your breath and deeply engaged with the struggles of your very human lives.

At every opportunity, know and celebrate both. My coming in the flesh was my Father speaking "baby talk" to this world's people. He was accommodating to your creaturely limitations so that you might come to know the unknowable and receive close-up the very far away. That's who I am and why I'm here. Celebrate the glory now come to you from the skies high above.

It's time for God's people, my people, to sing a new song! No more dirges or laments. Now that I have come and you know me personally through my Spirit, it's to be songs of praise because God has done truly marvelous things. The seas have begun roaring and the hills singing, with the floods of your praise to have no boundaries. God's right arm has dipped down into space and time (Ps 98). Worship with excitement as you come to understand this grand truth (Jn 4:24). Sing psalms, hymns, and spiritual songs with all your minds and hearts (Col 3:16).

24

BOTH CHRISTIAN AND PATRIOT? DIFFICULT!

My undergraduate college proudly promotes the school motto *Pro Christo Et Patria* ("For Christ and Country"). Jesus said we are to give to God what belongs to God and to the government what belongs to it. Doesn't everything belong to God? Can Christians be truly loyal to both God and country at the same time? Being good citizens of the powers here below must not be allowed undercut a Christian being a loyal citizen of the heavenly kingdom.

How far can a believer in Jesus go in fulfilling human expectation and that believer not be undercutting heaven's ultimate reign? This is a difficult question when social circumstances go very sour and a human government demands ultimate loyalty. What happens when a nation calls one to war and Jesus calls to seeking peace and reconciliation in his loving manner?

I once created an extended conversation among great Christian thinkers who proceeded to answer such questions somewhat differently.[113] They had known the worst and sharpened their contrasting views. They were Dietrich Bonhoeffer, James H. Cone, C. S. Lewis, James Earl Massey, Thomas Merton, Thomas C. Oden, and David Elton Trueblood, with me as moderator. Quite a line-up. Quite a subject!

Contrasting Voices

The background of the life experiences represented in my conversation was World War II, the Vietnam war, and the Civil Rights movement in the United States. The constant questions were these. When if ever is anger to be in the voices and whips and guns in the hands of the followers of Jesus? Can one be a disciple of Jesus and a patriot of a wayward earthly nation?" Aren't all earthly nations wayward? Here's a little of the conversation.

D. Bonhoeffer--I think of my time at the Benedictine monastery. I worked there on my book *Ethics* trying to understand and explain an ethical basis for being involved in the resistance against the Nazis. I knew that at some point I likely would be performing extreme actions, even political assassination. I was trying to justify such a thing as a responsible Christian person. Participating in a bloody overthrow of the Third Reich as a Christian is indeed a demanding thing to think through!

T. Oden—My early pacifist spell was broken by the uprising in Hungary and the ugly repression that silenced that freedom attempt in Eastern Europe. As I watched students resisting tanks, I realized that unjust power had to be met with justified resistance. Those intrepid students on the streets of Budapest offered me a model of courage completely different from my earlier pacifism. I realized that moral decisions require more than theories and ideas. So, Dietrich, I thoroughly understand the tough decision you made in resisting Hitler with more than holy abstractions.

T. Merton--I didn't go that way, brothers. I faced the same evil, Nazism, in the 1940s. I concluded that what Hitler represented could not be defeated by the same violent methods it used, raw power. The only adequate Christian response was sanctity. There is only one defense and that's to take the gospel literally and be serious "saints." Our spiritual lives must function and grow in the midst of our messy earthly realities. Despite the difficulties of life in the political arena, the church must work within the wideness and wildness of God. I sought to disappear into God, me a pacifist and monk with my own brother part of a bomber crew in the Royal Canadian Air Force. We did God's work differently.[114]

C. S. Lewis--We find ourselves as Christian believers always experimenting with how best to live effectively as Christians where we are. The practical problem of Christian politics is not that of drawing up schemes for a Christian society but of living as innocently as we can. As believing subjects, we always live under unbelieving rulers who will never be perfectly wise and good. That's why I lamented the need for violent resistance against the Nazis. Still, I feel forced to affirm the possible Christian legitimacy of such a stance because of the sheer necessity posed by that gross evil.

E. Trueblood--Christians like yourselves can create a reasonable case for a "just war," although others of us continue to struggle with that possibility being an acceptable expression of the Jesus life we meet in the Gospels. I admit that there is the paradox of the unloving pacifist who condemns all of those in the armed forces. Christian pacifism is a needed witness, but when separated from the love of Christ, it becomes cruel and bitter. Our choices as Christians are not predetermined, but I chose pacifism.

D. Bonhoeffer—Let me list our Christian choices. There are three ways for the church to respond to a society that has given itself over to evil. It can try to help the state by actively questioning its wayward actions. It can go further by actively assisting the victims of state actions, and for me that included the Jews. Then there's the boldest step I finally felt forced to take. The church might go beyond bandaging victims lying under the state's wheels. It might feel obligated under a just and loving God to jam a rod into the spokes of those wheels to save the mass of other soon-to-be victims. For me, the perversely spinning wheel was Hitler and I finally tried to jam a rod for the sake of humanity.

C. S. Lewis—People often judge from their armchairs without having been in the game. The boldness of your third step, Dietrich, seems too far to go, unless of course you were there. Saint Paul appears to approve of capital punishment when he says that the magistrate can bear the sword (Rom 13:1-7). When our Lord himself praised the centurion, he never hinted that the military profession was sinful in itself. This has been the general view of Christendom. Pacifism is a recent variation. We must, of course, respect pacifists, but I think their view is erroneous.

J. Massey--Christian citizenship always is to be primarily in the kingdom of God. My involvement in the American Civil Rights movement and friendship with Martin Luther King, Jr., involved a deep commitment to non-violence. I promote reconciliation without ignoring injustice. God's kingdom is not advanced by human violence. Peacemaking is the way to shape the best future. Those who do this work of reconciliation are God's true children. Even so, I admit that there seems to be limits to unqualified pacifism. When a Jew-exterminating Nazi is on the loose, the New Testament gives a mixed view of Christians relating to human governments. Joined is a sober realism about the roots of power, the fruits of idolatry, and a stern call for Christians to be keenly aware and ethically responsible.

J. Cone--Too often salvation is understood by Christians as only a mystical communion with the divine to get one to heaven and out of the horrors of the present. Oppressive societies are glad for such an escapist understanding. It makes religion an opiate that keeps people from challenging injustice. The gospel is a story of God's solidarity with the poor, empowering them in the fight for freedom. Blacks have sung songs about heaven, but it did not change the present state. We may walk one day in the promised land, but we want to walk in this land of the free and the home of the brave. Surely to believe in the God who creates heaven for us later is also to believe that such a liberating God doesn't want us to accept passively a hell on earth.

B. Callen--Friends, you have made clear a difficult paradox. God is love *and* righteousness. We are made very uncomfortable because of the frequent realities of our human nations. For Christians, is it God *and* country? The answer depends in part on what the country is about at any given time. Sometimes hard ethical choices must be made by those faithful to Jesus. You each have made differing choices in your Christian lives, each for thoughtful reasons. May God help and forgive us as necessary.

Is "Holy War" Really Holy?

Does the church create witnesses for the *next* world while not producing heroes of action for *this* world? Could Christianity be a *spiritual* success and a *social* failure? We must engage in public life as responsible citizens while carefully listening to the Spirit of God. We will not hear the same answer from the Spirit. Conscience must be followed. Keep us close to you, Lord, show us the way, and keep us patient with each other as differing believers.

What does *"Deus Vult!"* now mean for Christians.? This "God wills it!" was the historic Christian cry of the European crusades of the eleventh and twelfth centuries against the Muslims of the Middle East. The knights cried out, with swords swinging, that "we must recapture the holy places of our faith in the name of Jesus!" We hear echoes of this cry today in the United States from Christian "nationalists." They say we must take back our nation from the "secularists." But take it at what cost and in what manner?

Those crusades of long ago were bloody indeed and eventually failed in their objective. Is any "holy war" really "holy"? Is sitting on the sidelines and doing nothing holy? Is dominating our culture and forcing Christianity on others the goal and way of Jesus? Jesus said he was a very different kind of king and his kingdom was not of this world (Jn 18:36). Where does that leave believers politically? Should his servants ever fight? Should Jesus have come off that cross and slaughtered the soldiers ready to nail him? Help us Lord to understand better who you are and thus who we should be![115]

****

Jesus with the Final Word

(in part a paraphrase of Rom 13 and Rev 13)

Friends, put down the sword and do my Father's business my Father's way. Peter had questioned how I was choosing to be the Messiah, saying, "I'll use a sword if you won't!" (Mk 8:32). I told him he'd never know what it means to be my follower until we got straight how I was insisting on being the Messiah. To know God involves knowing that God's presence is hidden in the world's suffering. Love is not always painless but a path of servanthood. The first thing to do is seek my kingdom and righteousness (Matt 6:33). While giving to Caesar what little belongs to him, never forget what is first priority.

What's the place of the church in the political process? Fully compliant? Active influencer? Underminer? Totally separate? The answers are caught in the paradox of the thirteens (Rom 13, Rev 13). Paul calls the Roman believers to be responsible citizens of their nation. However, my followers should recognize that sometimes political powers emerge like a beast that is determined to devour the church (Rev 13). When that happens, ultimate loyalty must be to my Father. Like for me, that could mean ultimate sacrifice. Read again an insightful modern letter from prison.[116]

25

A HOLE IN THE ROOF? NO DOUBT!

A common way of measuring adequate living is to have at least a good roof over your head. It keeps out the harsh elements of nature and brings a certain level of security beneath its welcome shield. Time, however, has a way of eroding roofs. We humans are very fragile beings, as are the structures we build.

How do holes in the roofs of church life originate and finally get repaired? It may involve more than a hammer and a few nails. What about the possibility of using a hole constructively in the meantime? A few friends once managed it when they couldn't reach Jesus through the doors. There's always hope of redemption, a way of managing despite the leaky cracks and jammed entrances.

A report on "Space Tourism" once caught my attention. Billionaires are blasting off to have the unique experience of zero gravity and seeing Earth from fifty miles high. One said he was anxious to go where "the limitless grandeur of space" would render the harsh realities of daily life down here "almost meaningless and unimaginable."

That's nice if you are an escapist billionaire and can pay for the ride. Even if you are, the ride is only temporary. What about the obvious breakdowns in church life, the holes in the roofs not escapable by any expensive ride?

Fractured Lives

Everything down here in the gravitational world is vulnerable to disease, rust, wear, even death. The Bible makes two things clear. One is the fragility of our human existence. The other is the power of God to restore regardless of circumstance. God always is at work and never trapped by gravity or the victim of time or any form of decay. When crisis comes, we humans are instructed to focus on the never-failing love and restorative power of God.

A major hole had developed in the personal life of the biblical psalmist (Ps 41). Everything had gone wrong and was leaking out of control. "My sins have torn me to pieces and my enemies are wishing the worst for me" (41:4). Turning to God was the only hope left.

When things also had gone very wrong, Job had learned that "friends" can be very off base in their judgments, regardless of good intentions (Job 19). Jesus later would look down from the cross and see that most of his disciples were absent or looking on only from a safe distance (Mk 15:40-41). They were confused, seeing nothing but the huge hole in their highest hope.

The prophet Isaiah was aware of the consequences of the sinfulness of God's people (Isa 43:18-25). Human hearts were sick indeed and their wrongs piled right in God's face, the very One who so loved them and eventually would be their judge. There remained, however, the amazing divine love that intended to salvage and restore the breakdowns of Israel. This is still the one hope of the church and her members. Isaiah blesses Israel with the promise that God will do a new thing one day, providing a fresh way into a different and repaired future.

Life can get so fractured, full of holes, some not of our own making. Even so, there's good news. "I will make a way in the wilderness and rivers in the desert" (Isa 43:19). Exile was a huge fissure in the roof of Israel's history. The people were blindsided by despair and overwhelmed by their growing inability to see God working in the unwelcome world around them.

That had to end. It would! Our lives are full of limitations, leaky cracks, failures, sins with no excuse. Sometimes there seem to be holes in our roofs that aren't even there. We imagine the worst and worry needlessly.

God's Promises are Sure

Paul was recognized as a reliable voice of God in ancient Corinth, that is until some of those believers became convinced that he wasn't (2 Cor 1:18-22). The apostle was reminded critically that he had cancelled a promised visit, and for that his integrity was now in question. He was accused of being an apostate apostle! This threat to Paul's ministry inevitably undermined the Corinthian's confidence in the very gospel message he had preached. For this reason, Paul's response was vigorous.

God's promises are "Yes!" There always is a fix, a definite hope for redemption. Our response always should be "Amen," hope accepted, grace gladly received! The Spirit of God is at work assuring disciples that God's revelation in Jesus Christ never changes whatever their view of any particular preacher or action of a limited leader. This is the message Paul had delivered initially in Corinth. It could still be counted on to remain the truth and fulfill its promises regardless of storms, rumors, questionable circumstances, and other kinds of leaking church roofs.

Maybe praying is what's needed most. One day the roof over the sanctuary where you worship will develop a leak, or maybe it will be a big crack in your body. Someone will betray or a fond hope will crash to the ground. What then? Try this prayer.

> O God, stop me from finding someone to blame and instead be part of getting the problem fixed. Even if we Christians sit in our supposedly safe sanctuaries and sing "There Will Be Showers of Blessing," we must not ignore stains of rainwater already showing on the ceiling. I know I should quit worrying about my latest pain or fearing I will be forgotten when I die. Help me, God! Give me eyes to see beyond the immediate crisis. Let me glimpse the riches of your grace that go beyond the holes to the healings.

The hymn "Leaning on the Everlasting Arms" has been sung by Christians since 1887.[117] There are wonderful gospel truths throughout its verses. It's marching music for believers needing reminded that God is with us every step of our journeys. The third verse highlights the inner peace made possible because of the constant presence of Christ regardless of anything. Inspired by Deuteronomy 33:7 and Jesus' command to "Fear Not," the biblical way should be a path without dread that leans on Jesus in all things.

God's holiness is a central biblical teaching. God is not ordinary, common, human, but is unique, absolute perfection and purity. This otherness should inspire in us a radical awe. Regardless of circumstance, it should yield a constant "Nevertheless!" God's presence seeks to relate redemptively, hoping to share the divine life and holiness with us humans. Today, however, there is a problem, a hole in the Christian quest for such communion with and participation in the divine life.

The Cost of True Discipleship

Too many sermons are basically self-help seminars on becoming a better you. Churches, even in the holiness tradition, have tried hard to keep up with generic "evangelicalism" for the sake of numerical growth. Too often they have sacrificed their distinctive call to preach holiness.

In a culture of consumerism, preaching what people want to hear is easier than preaching the high cost of true discipleship. What gets muffled and causes power to leak away is loss of the optimism of personal transformation inherent in the Wesleyan-Holiness message of the higher Christian life.[118] Repair is urgently needed.

There now are holes in the roofs of the faith that we can't keep ignoring. How odd that Palm Sunday, with its triumphal parade into Jerusalem, has such an ominous underbelly. The triumph being shouted by the excited crowd soon would turn ugly and come at a high price not expected or wanted.

Viewing this Jerusalem scene from the immediate hours of its happening reveals only the crowd waiving their palms, the gleaming Temple, and the great joy in the streets. Looking back over the generations of God's people alters the picture considerably. Behind this day was the long trail of tears and frustrated expectations stretching over centuries. A brief view ahead would reveal the coming garden of arrest and then a cross of torture and death. Our salvation wouldn't come cheaply.

Who knows what awful things may lie ahead for any of us? How can the larger realities be seen and the big holes fixed or at least survived? While we waive excitedly the palm branches of the moment? May we not shy from the challenges of the difficult pathways likely ahead. Things are broken and we are being sent on fixing missions with Jesus.

There's no cheap grace—it cost the Lord everything! Division in the church is a scandal that can't be tolerated. Unholy people aren't effective representatives of a holy God. Let any who boast do so only about the Lord who alone is worthy (1 Cor 1:31). The many deficiencies of church life are redeemable only by the power of the Spirit of God being welcomed in its midst.

****

Jesus with the Final Word

(in part a paraphrase of Mark 2:1-12)

Do remember, my friend, one circumstance prominent in my earthly ministry. It required an extraordinary effort to reach my presence. The crush of the crowd forced four men of faith to cut a hole in the roof of a house where I was teaching. They were determined to face their dilemma with creativity and faith.

They squeezed a paralyzed man through the new hole on a stretcher and lowered him down into my presence. I saw the man and their great faith. While they were anxious for a bodily healing, I responded first with forgiveness of the man's sins, his deeper need. Always look beyond the moment to the deeper need and trust my judgment. Some in the crowd got upset that I dared claim the right and power to forgive sin. They didn't know who I was in relation to my Father. Do you? My disciples must first learn my identity before limiting the possibilities or judging my actions. The understandings of many people are full of holes.

I wasn't suggesting by what I did in that house that the man's sin had caused his paralysis. Neither was I suggesting that there never is any connection between the two. My people were being severely exploited by a brutal military power, taxed into poverty and desperation. This can cause physical and even mental breakdown. Whatever is causing the holes in your existence, your task is to get to me and let me decide about future possibilities.

26

WHEN THERE ARE NO RULES? LOVE!

Jesus loved his Jewish heritage but proceeded to transform it in significant ways. One change was to dispense with many of the religious rules of the Elders when good sense or human compassion suggested acting otherwise. He said that an adequate fulfilling of the Law of God is always practicing the *law of love*.

Many of life's situations have no clear rules to follow. Many issues are rising today that are unprecedented. Love always is available when set rules don't exist. Can you hear Jesus saying this? "Friends, we're wilderness bound. There are crosses to be carried and questions that will not be answered in advance. It will take creativity couched in genuine love. Are you coming? Don't ever forget the love!"

Clear rules of life's twisting and ever-changing road bring a kind of assurance. The problem is that often they don't exist. Law requires little thought, just doing whatever is required and moving on. The servant of God, however, is to be an instrument of the Spirit of God. That requires thinking and acting however the Spirit directs in each new circumstance. Being a divine instrument requires a receptivity to divine guidance.

Sometimes being a disciple of Jesus calls for the courage to follow experimental and unexplored paths regardless of resistance encountered or the danger of getting lost. It's not always possible to look in a book for the most relevant rule written in a much earlier time and in a very different cultural setting.

The Time Before Guidelines

The struggle between law and freedom fills the pages of the New Testament. Paul heralds a fresh freedom in Christ and is criticized by some as a worldly and dangerous libertine. He understood the gospel of Christ to be marked by freedom, gratitude, and joy. It's the life of "I want to do this because of Christ" rather than "I will do this because the Scribes and Pharisees say I must."

On the one hand, Christians are to live as resurrection people with an infectious testimony of joy and good news for all people.[119] On the other hand, the freedom and spontaneity of such living have no set rules reporting in advance how to do things in each new circumstance. Still, there is no such thing as absolute freedom. What then is one to do when free and yet not having the necessary rules for guidance?

The Bible walks a fine line between the perspectives of Romans 7 and Psalm 19. The Law "held us captive" and yet is "sweeter than honey." Which is it? The Galatian believers in Jesus lived in a world where the guidance we Christians now take for granted was brand new or didn't yet exist so far as they knew. Missing were historic Christian customs, rituals, set worship patterns, a calendar for community celebration, denominational "disciplines," even a written Scripture beyond the Old Testament. How were they supposed to act in such a vacuum?

As a pioneering first-century community of faith, early Christians lived with little tradition to ground their experience, especially the Gentile Christians who lacked any Jewish background. It was like playing football with no sidelines to the field. It's difficult to know when you're out-of-bounds. How do you argue with officials when you know they are making up the game's rules as play proceeds?

First-century Christians, and all of us today, need the assurance of clear rules of faith's road, but only if they are centered in the freedom of Jesus, as sweet as honey, and directed by love. Christian discipleship enjoys freedom of old human restrictions and yet requires both right beliefs and proper behaviors. If the Jewish law and the "traditions of the Elders" are no longer the safeguards against sin and the misuse of freedom, what is?

Paul responds this way. "Live by the Spirit and do not gratify the desires of the flesh." There is one law, the law of love mediated by the Spirit of love. The whole of the law of God is summed up in a single commandment. "You shall love your neighbor as yourself" (Gal 5:14).

While God calls disciples of Jesus to freedom, Paul announces a necessary caution. "Do not use your freedom as an opportunity for self-indulgence" (Gal 5:13b). "Sanctification" is not asceticism (denying ourselves to death) or athleticism (working ourselves to death). It's an acceptance that allows God's Spirit to love us into new life, abundant life, and finally everlasting life.

The indwelling Spirit of God, once accepted, motivates believers to engage the world with the hope of returning it to a necessary "holiness." It's a wholeness of life grounded in love. We are always to act with such motivation and in that direction. It must be recognized that the Bible is not intended to be a book of detailed instructions of exactly how to be holy in every time and place and circumstance. It's more an invitation to enter into an ongoing relationship and dialogue with God's Spirit about what God expects and love requires from time to time.

Discipleship is less indoctrination into a set of intellectual particulars and more an ongoing walk with Jesus and his people, constantly learning and serving because of and on behalf of that relationship. God is beyond full comprehension, beyond being captured in any theological formula or fixed set of rules for what to do in each life situation that may arise. God is rich in mercy and sacrificial love. God's people should be likewise.

What Is the Christian GPS?

What about when there is no clear memory of past guidance about what to do in a novel set of circumstances? What should happen when a decision must be made and there is no map, no precedent, only wilderness and an open road with no Christian GPS known to be available? The psalmist answers, "I bless the Lord who gives me counsel" (Ps 16:7). Beyond the church and Bible, especially when there are no guiding rules, we need to rely on the holy love and present ministry of God's Spirit.

Always relevant is this statement of Paul. "The only thing that counts is faith working through love" (Gal 5:6). Constantly heeded should be this demanding call of Jesus. He was so honest with potential disciples. When they weren't sure and wanted to delay decisions and mission, not sure of the best timing and rules and likely outcomes, Jesus said sharply, "Let the dead bury the dead. Get on with the work of the kingdom of God or stop talking about it. You are apostles who are wilderness bound. There are crosses to be carried and unknowns ahead. Are you coming or not?" (Matt 8:22).

Here's the proper picture of a committed Christian believer. All the known commandments of God are kept with all one's might. Obedience is known to be judged in proportion to God's love motivating one's service. The body and soul are presented without reserve as a living sacrifice (Rom 12:1). We are to proceed by devoting ourselves to God's glory and not our own, and by loving others as we do ourselves.

Negative stereotypes have gathered around "holiness" and "pentecostal" Christians, some deserved and some not. Such believers sometimes have said, "Follow the 'method' and get the assured result, instant sanctification or a dramatic spiritual gift or desired miracle. Just come and it will be done.

Regardless of faith being expressed in such mechanical obedience, Christianity is not a matter of putting the right password in the divine cash machine so that out will come the graces, gifts, and specific divine guidance needed. We can't buy the rules we think we need to follow. There isn't an "app" available with all the quick answers.

Christian holiness is essential, although not primarily the result of our efforts, discipline, or faithfulness. There is no sure result from chanting any set formula. Pride and arrogance over spiritual achievements or the possession of superior gifts are always inappropriate. Christian life flows from divine grace and is not measured by human works. Its genius is an inward holiness that can bring solutions and not more problems. That inwardness is itself a gift of divine grace.

Honoring the Law of Love

The Spirit of God is an active presence interpreting daily the meaning of the divine law of love. The Spirit is enabling loves proper fulfillment as life proceeds in the best ways we find possible. Such enabling revives the soul, makes wise the simple, and rejoices the heart. It transforms a law-oriented restrictiveness into something "sweeter than honey and more precious than gold" (Ps 19:10). Still lacking all answers, at least it's clearly the best way to walk.

At its heart, the law of God comes down to loving God and neighbor (Matt 22:37-39). Christian truth does not change but times do, making it necessary on occasion to rethink some of faith's language and life expressions. On the specifics of these changes we will not all agree. No matter. Love holds communities of faith together without there being a complete uniformity of thinking and acting.

John Wesley's whole approach to Christian theology was built around the central theme of love to God and others. His thought is like a great rotunda with archway entrances all around. No matter which is entered, it always leads to the central Hall of Love. Looking upward toward the dome, one gazes into the inviting sky since there is no ceiling to love. It serves to link every doctrine together into one beautiful dynamic."[120]

Here, then, is the proper Christian song and prayer. "That blessed law of Thine, Jesus, to me impart; The Spirit's law of life divine, O write it in my heart!"[121] This writing comes from the realization that the very nature of God is love itself.[122]

One wise woman once said it all. "Love takes the harshness out of holiness, the incredibility out of perfection, the moralism out of obedience, and the abstraction out of truth. Another wise woman cautions that a disciplined life of love is hardly automatic with the act of believing. "Most of us need habitual practices that daily open our hearts and minds to God's transforming love. Without regular reminders we tend to drift away from God's missional call to love and serve our neighbors."[123] In other words, there's to be no ducking of discipline in the name of the freedom of love!

****

Jesus with the Final Word

(in part a paraphrase of Luke 13:10-17)

Some religious leaders treat their animals better than their desperate neighbors. Beware of setting rules that benefit yourself and demonize others. If you find yourself having to step outside artificial rules to do the redeeming work of my Father, do it with love, but do it. When there is a cost, even from fellow disciples who won't understand, pay it gladly.

Be my agents of relational love in action whatever the circumstance. The Sabbath rules of my people were very fixed and clear, and yet on occasion I broke some of them. Technically, I was wrong. Actually, I was right. You must learn that human rules that claim to define what constitutes holy actions are fragile at best. Sometimes fellow believers will hold you accountable to a standard not necessarily mine.

Love must reign regardless. You can't know it all in advance, friends, you just can't. Love often will have to be flexible and experimental in application. My Spirit won't give you a book of fixed rules, only a divine presence who is prepared to show you the best way, one step at a time. Stay close to my Spirit. Thrill in the freedom of relationship with me. Never take it for granted or use it for your private purposes.

27

THE CHURCH'S FUTURE? GUIDELINES!

So much church life is experimental, adjusting to the times and people involved. Present times seem more challenging than ever. How is the church to stay on track and even survive? We can proceed believing this. "A Christian has no reason to be intimidated in the presence of today's later-stage 'modernity.' Christianity has seen too many 'modern eras' to be cowed by this one."[124]

It's wise to keep in mind five guidelines for the future. They won't answer everything in advance but at least they will keep the church moving, and always in the right direction. It may be that our times are so empty of solutions that mature faith in Christ may be seen in a surprisingly bright light. Are we back to life as it was in the early church, a tiny minority against impossible odds? Its success was considerable!

The times now are critical of the church and fast pushing it to the sidelines. There are at least a few guidelines for the church to follow in a future full of this degrading. They form something of a tract for transitional times.

The year 2000, dawn of a new century and millennium, was a particular moment of concern about what remains worthy of guiding the church of Jesus into a dramatic new future. Our human expectations and fears often are wrong. We are to relax and move on with at least a few dependable guidelines in hand.

There had been so much ugliness in the twentieth century. Was there even more to come in 2000 and beyond? Was a better corner being turned? We now have managed awkwardly the first twenty-five years of the new millennium and the search for the big things like peace, justice, and faith is still on with no good end yet in sight.[125]

Trustworthy Biblical Guidelines

For the church of Jesus in the years yet to come, there are no guarantees, only a few trustworthy biblical guidelines. The church is called to lean successfully into the better future God intends for his people. These guidelines for wise leaning are always to be kept in mind.

1. God's Time. Daniel Warner was the primary pioneer of the Church of God (Anderson) Movement begun in the late nineteenth century. He and his colleagues were called "flying messengers" with an urgent word of judgment and good news for the church and world of their time. They were sure it was a period of God's special working, even the soon-coming of Christ. There had to be a dramatic preparation for the Groom coming shortly for his Bride. These prophets were right about some things and obviously wrong about others. It's hard to read the signs of the times and stay perfectly on track. Preparation of the church was something they got really right.

In the late 1880s God was active in the life of the church on behalf of its renewed holiness, unity, and mission. Still today that divine initiative continues, maybe at an accelerated pace. We believers struggle with maps and calendars, expectations and accountability. Experienced holiness and Christian unity no doubt are closely related and urgently needed at all times. Church leaders again need to be flying and hopeful messengers of God's coming better day.

When is God's time? It's always *now*! I once dared to write on "end times," highlighting the constant importance of the present time and de-emphasizing fruitless speculation about supposed knowledge of the coming tomorrow.[126] Learn from yesterday and hope for tomorrow—but *live for today*! What time is it? It's *always* God's time.

2. A New World. What's this "post-modernism" that supposedly defines out days now? Its meanings are still emerging as it seeks to reshape our times. At least it's a repudiation of some of the unfortunate preoccupations of many church people in recent generations. These misguided preoccupations include the temptation to focus on mandatory theological systems, feature the power of human reason to know and "prove" the truth, and insist on rigid doctrinal propositions and revered religious institutions. Such past preoccupations now are being "deconstructed."[127]

Authentic Christianity requires faith, grace, and inner transformation. A holy church community makes room for necessary mystery, diversity, and spiritual growth. It's time for the church to look beyond the rigidities and fixed patterns of "modernism."

Resisted now must be common compromises of the hurtfully institutionalized and tragically divided Christian world of yesterday and today. Dynamic new life in God's Spirit needs to be the central reality of church life. It's God's church. The members are not finally in charge, nor are our thoughts, formulas, and institutions.

3. On "Seeing" the Church. Ever since the Protestant Reformation of the sixteenth century there has been an unfortunate Protestant emphasis on the "invisible" church. This evasive view has lowered the vision of God's intention for the church in the world. The accepted invisibility is justified by a range of "isms," including rampant denominationalism and an abortive individualism among believers. It's time to restore the ancient Christian emphasis on the "visible" church.

God intends the public to *see* a very real and united family of new creatures in Christ who are leading holy lives and pursuing together a holy mission. The "sectarian" spirit among contemporary Christians is to be repudiated. Walls among believers must be reduced to picket fences through which we can at least see and touch and love each other as believers.

Let's enable the public to start "seeing" the church, the whole of it, the unity of it, its beauty and eternal dimensions. Effective evangelism requires moving from good talking about the church to *being* the church in its intended holiness and unity. It's to be visible to ordinary "unchurched" people. Impact will come less from argumentation and more from visible demonstration. One church historian has caught this vision of the church that God intends.[128] Have you seen it in action? People judge by what they see, and the church must stop putting forth unfortunate images of itself.

4. Biblical and Apostolic. Today's non-church thought is certainly right about one thing. There is no such thing as a detached observer or an unbiased interpreter. Creedal and denominational arrogance is unwarranted. All believers should be humble and journey together in their growing understandings and sharing of the faith. No group has a corner on truth, not even your church. Authority lies in biblical revelation and apostolic teachings as ministered to our current understanding by God's Holy Spirit.

The correct call is still "back to the blessed old Bible." Going back to the right past and doing it in community with the whole Christian tradition is a necessary way to go on to the right future. Note two essays in this collection that focus on why and how to read the Bible wisely. The book *Radical Christianity* isn't about getting extreme and publicly ridiculous but calls for the church to go back to the roots of the faith so that its present fruits are authentic.[129] The right roots are essential in any time for achieving the right fruits.

5. Spirit and Form. Today's anxious church reformers must not overact to the obvious abuses in organized Christianity. Many pioneers of the past have cried out against virtually all organization in church life. They have been right at least about starting with God's Spirit. Jesus said that disciples should wait and receive the Spirit's baptism, the Father's promise, before proceeding with their world mission (Acts 1:4-5).[130] Spirit goes before form, possession before attempting to share the possession.

There are two essential dimensions of church life, the *dynamic* (charismatic) and the *stabilizing* (continuity with the tradition of the whole church). Both are essential for the church to be fully herself and in full preparation for her mission. Believers in Christ are to be free in the Spirit and yet mutually accountable to each other in some reasonably structured manner. Form is necessary, although it's fragile and only to be a temporary vehicle for the life and work of the God's Spirit. Believers are to be alive in the Spirit and then thoughtful in planning church advance.

> O Jesus, I have promised to serve Thee to the end;
> Be Thou forever near me, my Master and my Friend.
> I shall not fear the battle, If Thou art by my side,

Nor wander from the pathway, If Thou wilt be my Guide.[131]

****

Jesus with the Final Word

(in part a paraphrase of Matthew 16:18)

Like the Jews of old wandering in the desert wilderness, you my dear disciples might be denied entrance into your promised land. To avoid such rejection, you must not cling to the security of the present. You must not long for the presumed joys of an idealized past. The writer to the Hebrews gets it right. "Today, if you hear the voice of the Holy Spirit, do not harden your hearts as in the day of testing in the wilderness" (Heb 3:7-8).

Fear freezes while faith follows on. I will continue to build my church. Its future is guaranteed, but not necessarily its organizations and rituals and creedal formulas. Things might come to look different than you expect or want. That's not the issue. The central fact is that the Body of Christ will never die! Times change, as do spiritual leaders and mission strategies. Even so, my Father is constant, available, adequate, and eternal.

Instead of standing on biblical promises, too often my people seem satisfied spending time just sitting on the church premises complaining and going through the usual motions. If you keep that up, promised lands will evaporate before our eyes. Can you trust my Spirit to be adequate for all your needs if you will dare to venture out on the divine mission? Indeed you can! You are nearly there. No stopping now. Don't fear tomorrow. Approach it in my name and in my way.

We've now asked a range of questions about the only church that is real, the one Body of Christ. It can be its true self only when holy and united. If this one church is faithful, stays anchored and refuses to die, what is the future ahead? It's amazing beyond words. Jesus always is given the last word!

28

WHAT IF GOD DOESN'T ANSWER? STAY ANCHORED!

I've prayed and cried and waited, but nothing has happened! No answer from above. Now what? Am I asking for the wrong thing, not being patient enough, not listening, haven't enough faith? Has God gone deaf? These are questions often faced by those who believe. Receiving no answer can bring a little panic when life's heat is turned high.

Instead of becoming discouraged, be patient and hold on. Mature faith will find ways to adjust to lingering mystery. Keep honoring and praising God and not insisting on answers coming strictly on your own timing or terms. The needed answer will come in proper time and be for the best. May we be protected from disillusionment by the depth and solid anchoring of our faith.

Have you seen the sign "Jesus Is the Answer!"? I've heard this response to it. "What's the Question?" People wonder. Is this the right time or not? There's never a good time. I can't marry yet. I need my career first. I can't believe yet because I still have unanswered questions and an unresolved past. I certainly can't die because there are so many things still to get done. One would-be disciple said to Jesus, "I'll follow you, *but not yet*. First, I have to get my kids raised and my parents buried" (Lk 9:60).

When used as excuses to avoid hard decisions, these are unacceptable delays in joining Jesus in his world mission. Often we don't have the time, means, or answers we think we need. One biblical prophet struggled when his big life questions seemed resistant to all available answers. He was tired of waiting on God to respond. He wanted a God who answers *now*. Does God sometimes answer and we aren't listening? Or might the answer be something we just don't want to hear?

Does God Have a Problem?

Does God suffer from Attention Deficit Hyperactive Disorder (ADHD)? An atheist understandably criticizes any God who claims to and but fails to meet all human needs, solve all problems, satisfy all desires, and answer all questions.

It's proper to critique the human tendency to self-serving fantasy. God is not a cosmic bellhop who gets all things done for us. The prominent biblical stress on divine judgment and the call for believers to be self-sacrificing address directly the atheist's understandable criticism.

We often insist, "God, please pay attention!" (Ps 5:1). God seemed hyperactive in the past, creating worlds, people, routing enemies, etc. Now, the psalmist was in trouble and no help was coming. Divine ears had turned deaf and powerful hands had become inactive. We believers occasionally find ourselves caught between Psalms 8 and 13.

We marvel at God's amazing creation and ask why God bothers with us (Ps 8:4). Then we suffer because of divine silence and complain, "Long enough, God. You've ignored me long enough!" (Ps 13:1). Is God off his meds? According to a Yiddish proverb, "God will provide, but oh that he would until he finally does!"[132] "O Lord, how long shall I cry for help and you will not seem to even listen?" (Hab 1:2).

The "why" and "how long" questions had become urgent when painfully unanswered. Would answers ever come? Had the Babylonian gods put the God of the Jewish tradition to sleep, rendered him helpless, deaf to the cries of his own people? How can "bad" people prevail while the good ones suffer, and with the powerful and good God presumably watching and seeming to do nothing about it?

There Are Partial Answers

Know at least this. We may be closer to God when asking hard questions than when parading arrogant and inadequate answers we think we have. There may be more genuine faith in honest doubt than in the blind believing of a merely conventional creed. Beware of church people who say the right things and do nothing about it. The prophet Habakkuk knew the pain of unanswered prayer and yet did receive some key answers from God (1:5-11, 2:2ff).

He realized, whatever the circumstance, that the Lord is from everlasting (1:12). God still is in his holy temple (2:20) and "enables me to go on to the heights" (3:19) regardless of limited understanding. The righteous must live by faith (2:4). Knowing that God *is* assures us that one day needed answers *will come*.

The Book of Job asks an obvious question and never receives its direct answer from God. He wanted to know why he suffered so much. Apparently, it's best to ask, "What are you trying to teach me, Lord, about the struggles of this life?" The lesson is this. God knows what He's doing, so we must trust when there are no "why" answers yet available. God's work and its final outcome are sure and just and definitely will be *wrapped in love*.

Here's an important point. We believers must judge things good or evil not by reference to the presently visible but by the invisible and eternal. Mature faith will adjust to lingering paradox and unrelenting mystery. We are to relax and leave room for God to act when and how it seems best to God. Divine thoughts and strategies are not always ours to know, at least not yet.[133]

> Jesus calls us o'er the tumult of our life's wild, restless sea;
> Day by day I hear him saying, "Christian, come and follow me."
> In our joys and in our sorrows, Days of toil and hours of ease,
> Still he calls in cares and pleasures, "Christian, love me more than these."[134]

Sometimes it's necessary to proceed in life and ministry without the answers. Yes, it's hard to live with ambiguity. Often what we need, however, aren't answers as much as an immovable rock on which to stand while questions remain unanswered.

> We have an anchor that keeps the soul,
> Steadfast and sure while the billows roll,
> Fastened to the rock which cannot move,
> Grounded firm and deep in the Savior's love.[135]

Intimate Relationship Avoids Disillusionment

That final line of the hymn quote is crucial. "Grounded deep in the Savior's love" is the intimate relationship that avoids disillusionment when answers to prayer haven't seemed to come. As we proceed in our study of the Bible, there is no way to predict what joyful discoveries and painful struggles we will experience.

This is the way of our life with God. It's a faith journey with the Spirit.[136] Mature believers in the biblical God learn to live with doubts and unanswered questions. It's part of the human condition and the biblical way. "Now I know only in part; then I will know fully, even as I have been fully known" (1 Cor 13:12). Faith fills the gap created by our continuing and sometimes painful ignorance.

When the Lord has not yet returned and horrific genocides still happen around the globe, can we believe in the all-powerful God of all goodness? Various answers are floated. None seem adequate. Can we learn from Job? We are not equipped to think God's high thoughts. Can we find comfort in going on without all the answers? Does Christian maturity include not needing to know what can't yet be known?

Habakkuk 3:2 is an ancient prayer worthy of repeating daily. The prophet stands in awe of God's past deeds and asks, "Renew them in our day, in our time make them known." Patience may be required if the answers that do come are somewhat different than the past deeds of God that we know. Even so, there is hope that soon "I will rejoice in the Lord." Why? Because "the Sovereign Lord is my strength" (3:18-19). Answers always will be consistent with the loving nature of God, who is from everlasting to everlasting.

Our personal prayer is to be this. "Lord, it's difficult to talk on your behalf until you first have talked to me. Help me recall and then stand in awe of your wonder-full works in the past. Then revive my present faith so that I can rejoice and make them known to others. Make my faith strong enough that I can go on believing even when I find it necessary to keep on asking. My precious Lord, protect me from disillusionment. Help me turn the struggle of unanswered prayer into an opportunity to grow in intimacy with you."

****

Jesus with the Final Word

(in part a paraphrase of Matthew 6:9-13)

You asked, my friends, that I teach you to pray. Here's prayer lesson number one. Start by honoring my Father. A fundamental human mistake is focusing primarily on personal needs and wants, often confusing the two. The twenty-first century encourages the "I's" to dominate. Whether I-Phone, I-Pad or a thousand marketing ads insisting on "my" rights and needs being met. The constant cultural standard is "I."

People are encouraged to live as though "we are" and God is not. Even people in my church are affected by this perverted preoccupation. An ideal citizen of my kingdom will make the first words of every prayer "Our Father." Begin by acknowledging the reign of God over all your fragile little kingdoms. You cannot pray my recommended prayer and focus on "I." You cannot say the Lord's Prayer and even once selfishly say "my." Nor can you fail to pray for another when you ask for daily bread, because this request must include reference to your brothers and sisters in need.

From the beginning to the end, my suggested prayer never once says "me" except to survive temptations.[137] Hallowing my Father's name is the place to begin when seeking answers to the troubles at hand. If no answer comes immediately, keep humbly honoring my Father and he will honor you. Ask to be rescued from the evil one who demands quick and desired answers and personal satisfactions.

29

THE BEST WAY TO DIE? DON'T!

Appearances can fool. A tree can be dead to the eye while its deep roots remain full of potential for new growth. What yet might be could be quite different from what once was or currently appears. For us humans, is new creation a possibility? Is death necessary? Is there a way we can avoid death altogether, now or at least hereafter?

The big news of the Christian faith is that we can escape death! While in this present life, we are invited to die and then not be dead but more alive than ever and remain so forever! It involves yielding ourselves into the life of Christ who is the Living Dead One. That yielding allows us to die to our sinful selves and receive the gift of eternal life.[138]

I love Galatians 2:20. "I have been crucified with Christ and I no longer live, *but Christ lives in me*. The life I now live in the body I live by faith in the Son of God who loved me and gave himself for me." Here is a summary of the good news in Jesus Christ, all that God has done for us lost sinners and what amazing newness now can come because of Jesus. Paul was testifies that he was very alive. He had been dead and now wasn't and never would be again!

The Illusion of Present Death

In an August, 1837, letter, Victor Hugo describes how he felt when first riding a train. He reacted with nervousness bordering on sheer terror. "I felt like a projectile, like a human parcel suddenly unhooked from reality and being sent to some far beyond." Was there impending death or just a false perception of danger?

The speed was faster than humans had ever before traveled on land. It train's motion seemed "to transform and even hallow the countryside into a mere blur. The flowers by the side of the road are no longer flowers, but streaks of red or white." Hugo's magical train was traveling at a reality-altering fifteen miles per hour!

Some eight decades later there were early automobiles, experimental, open to the air and said to be capable of traveling nearly twice as fast as Hugo's train. Beyond fascination at the outside views, true fear was being expressed. Surely in air moving that fast humans would not be able to breathe. On arrival, they surely would be dead of suffocation! Is the threat of death real but unnecessarily frightening?

Some things aren't at all how they appear at first. Fear on occasion is merely the result of our ignorance and lack of experience. What about time? The immediate and long-term can be very different. Tchaikovsky's *The Nutcracker* ballet was performed first in Russia (1892). Czar Alexander III was in the audience and loved it, but the critics hated it. The papers "reviled me cruelly," lamented Tchaikovsky. He died of cholera months later, never knowing that *The Nutcracker* would become an international success still loved today. Politicians have the problem of being very popular when first elected and soon detested because of this question. "What have you done for me lately?"

Some Surreal Months

The months of 2003 was surreal for me. Thy flew by and also seemed to stand still. That year began with the death of my beloved first wife and ended with my marriage to the second. Time had stopped and then suddenly accelerated. Here are three brief portions of my personal journal of that year.

February 27, Thursday. Tuesday night found me alone with Arlene, staying on the couch next to her and helping her nausea when it came, handling the ice pack changes every two hours. It appears that the end surely will come soon for her. She and I pray together, mostly giving thanks for God's goodness over the years (we've been married for nearly forty) and his many gracious helpers (Hospice nurses and others). We were asking for mercy with the pain and nausea.

Arlene said to me, "I want anything between us that needs to be forgiven to be so." We assured each other that all was well. She said she wanted me to feel no guilt about anything when she was gone. "I will try," I said, though surely there will be something else I could have done.

March 1, Saturday. Arlene just breathed her last. Minutes before the end I had leaned over and said in her ear, "Thanks for everything, Honey. We are all here and love you very much. If God is calling you home, feel free to go to your better place." Shortly after, she breathed very slowly, then quietly stopped, was calm and gone.

It was over. It had been a long and hard journey since the first cancer diagnosis last April, nearly a year, but finally Arlene had left the dark valley and journeyed into the great light of God's love beyond. For her, time had ended, or had it just begun? She had died, or had she?

September 21, Sunday. During the morning worship service at Park Place Church of God, I thought much about Arlene. Last March she had gotten what she wanted, free of her limitations and I being set free to marry someone who would love to travel the world with me. I reflected, "It has turned out as she wanted! Arlene is fully free and exactly three months from today I will be marrying as she had hoped. God is surprising and amazing! I have no words, only gratitude."

So it is with human life in general. How much we need the church and each other, especially in times of dramatic personal change. Time gets emptied and then refilled with the arriving grace of a loving God. How mysterious and yet wonderful are the ways of God. Death comes, and yet not really. We all are pilgrims still in progress, walking together by faith. For all that has been and yet will be, to God be the glory! Life somehow leads to life.

Jesus' Resurrection Is Ours!

What will be after death? Speed is relative. Perception can be misleading. Time is fleeting, maybe standing still, maybe just beginning. When death comes, does time stop for the deceased or only begin and even accelerate? My faith tells me that God was before time and will be after time has ended. This God of all eternities is in the business of resurrecting and re-creating. God brings to life that which is dead. God restarts the stopped life clocks of his dear children. God loved before we were conceived and will love far beyond what we now can conceive.

The Jesus story is about a cross and then an empty grave, his *and ours* (Jn 11:26). All our human stories should pivot around this story. A cross once stood on a hill outside old Jerusalem. The man hanging on it was soon dead, and then wasn't, and now walks among us quietly as the living and loving dead one. The Spirit of Christ, source of true life, extends a gracious hand and offers each of us a life that is eternal.

To be fully alive is to take that hand and walk humbly by the Spirit's side through this life and then into another yet to come. Christians go back to this baseline of all reality, the foretaste of a future promise to us that can be real even in the present (Gal 2:20).

Jesus *is* the living dead.[139] With him, death has lost its sting and has no lasting reality. To go forward, we must go backward to this baseline event. We must encounter the ever-livingness of the once but no longer dead man, Jesus. God is with us and forever for us in Jesus. He is the Eternal among the tombstones of we mortal humans. We should sing and pray: "Breath on me, Breath of God, so shall I never die, but live with Thee the perfect life of Thine eternity."[140]

Surely the wildest cemetery visit of all time is recorded in Ezekiel 37. Imagine yourself flying over a massive graveyard. You look down and see it spread across an entire valley of the desert floor. Nothing's been buried or even covered, just millions of bones, dried, bleached, and picked clean of all flesh. Your pilot makes a turn back for a second look. It's just as amazing a sight as the gruesomeness of the first time.

But wait! Something is happening, moving, frightening! Suddenly you see the unthinkable right before your eyes. All of those bones are moving, rattling and reconnecting. You shoot photos as fast as your camera will work. They won't believe this back home. The skeletons, thousands of them, are now neatly back together, with new flesh and breath, the *ruah* of God. They have become a new city of the living dead, dancing with joy on the desert floor.

How does that old song go? "Dem bones, dem bones, dem dry bones, now hear the word of the Lord." What's that word? It's that there really can be, somehow, someday will be a God-enabled resurrection dance of unbelievable proportions, and the joy of it all will be beyond description. It can start even today!

> Lives again our glorious King,
> Where, O death, is now thy sting?
> Dying once, He all doth save,
> Where thy victory, O grave? [141]

****

Jesus with the Final Word

(in part a paraphrase of John 12:20-33)

Her my own personal testimony, my friends. It's hardly the way of the world and certainly not the way I would have chosen for myself in my humanness. Put simply, my terrible death was the way of my Father's great love, and thus, painful or not, also my choice. I had to die to draw all people to myself (Jn 12:32). Now, my dear disciples, the only path for you is to faithfully follow me, losing life to really find it. Remember this. What you will lose is what should never have been in the first place.

I know this is hard to do or even understand. I've been there, experiencing the pain of your struggle (Heb 5:7-8). You now are dead in your sins. I am offering life that is eternal. I leave you with this jarring observation. A seed must die for it to bear much fruit (Jn 12:24). I call you to die to your sinful selves, receive my gift of eternal life, and follow me wherever I lead.

This death to one's selfish nature means deciding to never die, starting immediately! It's "eternal" life, meaning the quality of the life of my Eternal Father. Such life leads to a new world and extends beyond time as humans now know it. Drink in my life and you will never thirst again.

My dear disciple Polycarp faced martyrdom in Smyrna because of his unrelenting Christ-likeness and witness. He refused to recant, so they burned him alive. When the church recorded what happened, the glorious words were these. "Polycarp was martyred, Statius Quadratus being proconsul of Asia, and Jesus Christ being King forever!" That, my friends, is worth a big "Amen!" and "Hallelujah!"[142]

30

ARE THESE THE LAST DAYS? ALWAYS!

Some Christians in all generations of church history have believed that theirs was the last generation before Jesus would return to end all time and human history. We now know that, at least so far, all these expectations have been wrong. They have been right in one way. The New Testament says that all days are to be considered "the last." We already know *what* and *who*, just not *when*.

Jesus was very clear about our present agenda as believers. We are to get ready, keep your lamps filled with oil and shining. Today could be it. Meanwhile, what must be dominant in our minds is that Jesus *already has come*! The kingdom of God has been inaugurated. Waiting for its consummation is not to be a passive business. While waiting, we are to be busy about the Lord's present mission.

If the Christian hope is reduced to only the salvation of the soul in a heaven beyond death, it loses its power to renew life and change the world of today. Its flame is "quenched and it dies into no more than a yearning for redemption from this world's veil of tears."[143] Hope for the arrival of God's promised tomorrow should enhance and not undercut our responsibilities for today.[144] While this immediate responsibility is very real, it's hardly designed for the excitement of the popular social media.

No Calendar Provided

People in general prefer an excited grabbing of a current news headline and claiming to find it predicted in some isolated Bible verse. Hal Lindsey was one of the best-selling Christian book writers of all time.[145] He claimed to be giving God a chance to speak about the future instead of the "scholars" whom he claimed were influenced by non-biblical presuppositions.

Lindsey's own "non-fiction" works themselves slipped into the fiction category whatever his claim. Surely the marketplace success of books isn't a fair judge of what's really true. Public gullibility is counted on by the big marketing firms.

Jesus said that the way to destruction is very broad and on it many travel, even some supposed biblical proclaimers. They occasionally come up with fascinating theories that in fact are nothing but a fanciful twisting of current events paired with Bible misreadings. Lindsey, only a decade after his *The Late Great Planet Earth*, released another popular volume, *The 1980s: Countdown to Armageddon*. It carried a new political agenda and was criticized widely for its author being carried along by the winds of social change.

In fact, the Bible provides divine foundations, impulses, intents, and assurances about the future, but *not* calendars and grand political schemes with contemporary nametags. These come from our frustrations, fears, preferences, and imaginations. What was Hal Lindsey doing in the second volume? He was making significant adjustments since his earlier "prophecies" hadn't worked out as expected.

Unfortunately, we anxious believers can be more reflections of our times than proclaimers of God's actual revelation about today and tomorrow. What are the biblical "scholars" doing? I can't speak for them all, but this speaks for most I have known.

> The Bible is a massive text that is millennia old, composed in non-English languages, in cultures so different from ours, sometimes using styles of writing not familiar to modern readers, and at points based on assumptions of the ancient Middle East foreign to the Western mindset of today. If probing carefully and compensating for all that is being "scholarly," then so be it. Scholars are careful readers and interpreters because of their love for God's Word.[146]

Focus on the Big Truth

Let's focus on the big truth that gets around all distracting speculations. *Christ already has come!* Christian life is the result of that completed historical coming. It's fired further by awareness that the fulfillment of the intent of the first coming will be consummated one day by the final coming. In the meantime, Christians have a mission to accomplish, ground to gain, preparations to make.

One work presents competently the range of speculations of some Christians about the ultimate future.[147] All that aside, however, it's time to be active on behalf of the year that's now at hand. Disciples of Jesus must keep balanced and humble about our speculations that stray well beyond what the Bible has chosen to reveal. We must not build whole belief systems out of mere fragments of biblical materials taken out of context. Our being clever and able to sound convincing is no excuse for sloppy and self-serving biblical interpretation.

Too many Christian theologies put the subject of "end times" toward the conclusion of their writing. This is understandable but seriously misleading. It should be *at the beginning*. What will be already has begun to be and now is the launching of what the church is to be all about in advance of a second coming of Jesus, be that tonight or centuries away.

What was there at the beginning of the Christian movement that should bring into true focus our Christian todays and our future expectations? Just this. A beaten, broken, and deeply discouraged group of nobodies, the first disciples of Jesus, was transformed suddenly into vibrant and courageous proclaimers of the resurrection of Jesus. They launched the Christian faith community and remained faithful to their daring belief for the rest of their lives, often despite intense persecution.

What could possibly account for this dramatic shift from fear and discouragement to bold belief and proclamation? The answer is straightforward. Jesus in fact *had risen!* And there is more. Someday, as promised, they also believed that Jesus will return for us and we too will be raised! That's the heart of this whole end-times matter. We aren't told exactly when or how, only that it *will be* because God lives and loves and always is faithful! Since we already know *what* but not *when*, we must treat every day as the last.

Redeem the Remaining Time

Let's determine to aim at heaven, of course. Meanwhile, let's be committed to redeeming our remaining time here on earth. Let's plan to join the heavenly chorus that we are told cries out "Hallelujah! For the Lord our God, the Almighty reigns. Let us rejoice and exult and give him glory!" (Rev 19:6). However, in the meantime, let's be careful of rash speculations, being faithful in our present mission.

The message of the Book of Revelation was first directed to a situation of persecution threatening the Christian church with demands for emperor worship. Its teaching application is not limited to that time long ago or that specific challenge. John's prophecy can relate to situations in subsequent times that are anticipated by his visions.

This, however, doesn't justify our making one-to-one correlations between the original "prophecies" and crises in today's headlines. They apply only when they are similar to the original crises, not in name and date but in substance.

Any contemporary application of presumed biblical prophecy must be grounded in the past and then allowed to shed light on the present, but not as specific predictions of present particulars. Claiming any such predictions violates biblical integrity and has been hurtful and often a self-serving process in the church for centuries.[148] We so much want to know future particulars. We easily watch and listen and buy anything that claims immediate explanations of the coming tomorrow.

Whatever the details of the future's conclusion to life in this world, the Bible has one clear message on which we can depend. These days of our current living are the "last days" in a very real sense. Check Matthew 25:1-13. Some weren't paying attention, weren't prepared, had to scramble in desperation, and finally got locked out. Today, every day, has this as its agenda number one in God's eyes. Be ready! Be busy on my mission in the meantime!

We beloved children of God are being forming into the image of Christ and to be functioning selflessly as agents of Christ's reign in this present world. For how long? For however long this world or our lives in it endure. Inspired and strengthened by our faith in the world yet to arrive one day, maybe this day, we know at least that God's eternal community already has dawned, is continuing to dawn, and one day will arrive home in its fullness.

Before it does, whenever that is, we believers are to be about God's present business. Otherwise, the end could happen this very night, our lamps won't light because they are out of oil, and all the stores will be closed! Since we are to be constantly active in Christ's mission, and thus always prepared for judgment at any time, each day must be treated as the "last"! Hear Jesus carefully. Read again that tragic lock-out story in Matthew's Gospel (chap. 25).

****

Jesus with the Final Word

(in part a paraphrase of John 1:6-8, 19-28; 6:51-58)

Hear these words carefully, my friends. My first coming on the public scene was after the voice of John the Baptist had been heard by many. He was humble enough to brush off what people at first thought. John wasn't the arriving Messiah. He kept his ego under control and pointed to another, to me. His experience will always be a challenge for you disciples. When my Spirit gifts you and wonderful things follow, be careful what titles you enjoy, credits you accept, and supposed knowledge you claim to have from me.

The light of my Father is coming and you must be its faithful carriers. The Gospel of John begins not with stories about my birth but with grand statements about my presence with the Father before and at the original creation. I am before, during, and after time itself. You are privileged to be glimpsing the new creation I am bringing. It's the same heavenly light that shined before the origins of time. Rejoice in this and don't buckle under the pressure of any crowd.

I am the Alpha and Omega. Don't construct fanciful stories of what will come next. Just be busy for me and ready for my coming yet again. Know that "eternal life" is the truly fulfilling life that's not a blessing conferred merely at death. It's an endowment shared for your present lives of ministry in my name and by my Spirit. Live divine life *now*. If you do, I assure you that such divine life pulsating within will continue through death and far beyond. Knowing this is enough. Get ready and be ready. Think of every day as the "last."

When the end of time comes, I will be there to take you to your ongoing home.

31

WHAT'S HEAVEN LIKE? UNKNOWN!

Faith now sees ahead only dimly through frosted glass (1 Cor 13:12), but at least we believers can make out the face of Jesus. That's more than enough! What's coming eventually will be the completion of what's already begun. Our hope is for an extension of the eternal life now being experienced by divine grace.

Except for being extraordinary and fully satisfying, the details of heaven's nature are largely unknown and really don't matter. What matters is living in the meantime so that we will recognize things when we get there and truly belong. We will know then as we are known now. Advance knowledge isn't everything; advance preparation is. The One who has gone ahead is the One who will be waiting for our arrival. He already is well known to us. Jesus is pure love and right by our side![149]

All actual knowledge of heaven and the final events leading to it is speculation at best, except for four glorious facts that the great creeds of Christianity all affirm. Jesus will come again. There will be a resurrection of the dead and a final judgment. There will be everlasting life with God for those who chose in their lifetimes to be re-formed and reflect the life of the Spirit of God. The reign of God will be supreme and have no end. That's all, those four, and that's enough. The rest is speculation.

As the River Flows

The hymn writer, having composed four stanzas of the many things not now known by us, comes to the central wisdom of what is known, concluding with this:

> But I know whom I have believed,
> And am persuaded that God is able,
> To keep that which I've committed,
> Unto him against that day.[150]

In other words, knowing "Who" enables confidence in the future, whatever the details turn out to be. The Who, of course, is Jesus, resurrected, glorified, our friend and our future. Since his tomb is empty, ours also will be one day soon! Can you see birth embedded in death? To be able to see this is to know all that's necessary for now.

After the crucifixion of Jesus, his first disciples were sure the Romans were coming for them next. Instead, Jesus appeared in their midst. "I'm alive! I'm not horror but hope, not tragic yesterday but amazing tomorrow. Live without fear my friends. Get outside and get going. There's so much to be done, such a great story to tell!"

Jesus was talking about a new kingdom now arriving, the loving and redeeming reign of his Father. The "living dead" in Christ were being commissioned as gracious agents of needed change in a troubled world. They were to model life in this new kingdom and proclaim it to the world as they themselves journeyed on toward the world yet to come.

Disciples of Jesus know that what's coming eventually will be the completion of what already is. The hope is about an extension to others of the eternal life that's being experienced now. Christ's past resurrection is to be ours, the power and hope by which we believers can live now and until then. It's the light by which we can see ahead enough to enable the demands of present discipleship.

The first president of the Anderson University wrote a moving autobiography. He begins with this. "On long and lazy summer days, the Meramec River is the picture of peace and quiet and rest. I love to linger on her bank and hear the music of her waters. They seem to be singing about the meaning of things. Men have come and gone from her banks but she keeps rolling quietly along. And in her music there seems to be reason as well as rhythm."[151]

Wisdom is in such deep perceptions of the ongoing of life's waters. Love is threaded through the pages of human history, even if often unseen. Will we linger and hear? Jesus now has joined the flow for our ultimate well-being. To benefit from this, we must visit the banks of passing time and hear and see and believe. As the life river ever flows, there persist the resurrecting grace and power of the eternal God. Will we linger long enough to realize and be changed?

Following the Ever-Moving God

We hear Paul report good news of a crucified and risen Messiah who appeared to numerous witnesses (1 Cor 15:1–11). Jesus was not merely as some disembodied ghost (15:44). We naturally are full of questions. How are the dead raised? With what kind of body will they come? (15:35). Can such things really be? Whatever the future holds, can we find eternal life even before we die? Of course, we'll all die, but can we be divinely alive before that, and also long after that?

Sunrise symbolizes the very essence of God. God is new light, warming love, and arriving future, a new day, a new way, fresh hope. In the end, darkness will have no chance to survive the divine light. *The Message* paraphrase of the Bible renders the opening verses of the Gospel of John this way. "The Life-Light blazed out of the darkness; the darkness couldn't put it out!" It never has and never will.

God is the beginning and ending, the initial Creator and the eventual Re-Creator. Joy and future are woven into the very fabric of the creation. That for which we hope eventually will be! The joy that bubbled from God's heart and originally brought forth creation will find a way one day to turn our darkness into light. The night of death can and will become the dawn of a resurrection eternity. That gracious redemption already is active all around us. It waits our response and participation. It is our intended home. It is heaven below and then above.

Does yesterday necessarily define tomorrow? Are we doomed by defective genes, forever scared by our troubled childhoods, helplessly dead in our sins? No! The Jerusalem of tomorrow will be very different than anything today. It will be a golden city without walls. The Book of Revelation seeks to describe something yet beyond description. God is never trapped in or forced to repeat any yesterday. The church is to be moving on with the ever-moving God. Mature disciples of Jesus are to be less products of their families and times and more first fruits of the resurrection of Jesus, who is the coming of a new time that is in and beyond our time.

Spiritual resurrection brings new life that's sent on mission. The suffering of yesterday must not be allowed to swallow the big possibilities of tomorrow. Out of the ashes of a terrible fire can rise things quite unexpected. Testifies Paul, "It is no longer I who live, but Christ who lives in me" (Gal 2:20). Can any of us measure that? Can life lived in this amazing way be limited to what losses have troubled our yesterdays or what things we fear may doom our tomorrows? God is moving and making all things new (Rev 21:5).

More Marvelous than Expected!

Look at what the carpenter Jesus made from the rough wood of his own cross. Human hate became divine love. What might God help us make out of our aloneness, grief, and frustration? Crucifixion can be construction. Death can be the opening to life.

Whatever the new Jerusalem of tomorrow is to be, it will be different from the old city, good as it was in some ways. The Bible speaks of the new city. God has moved into the neighborhood. Jerusalem is resplendent as never before, shining with newness, a bride finally ready for her husband. God will inhabit that tomorrow, making it a divine residence for his beloved children. Jesus will be there with keys in his hands. They open and lock death's doors and hell's gates (Rev 1:18). They make heaven's doors swing wide open.

While there are many unknowns about tomorrow, known indeed is the One who holds the future, who builds the new city, whose heart is known to be love. Whatever tomorrow's heavenly details, its depth and dimensions already are known. Check the empty cross and grave of Jesus and jump with joy! Pray for assurance during life's long hours and dark nights. God has spoken protection from whatever may be lurking in the darkness. The call is to patience until the final dawning of God's morning light.

The same Christ who has died and risen for us and will return to raise us to the joys of life eternal. Little is known about this eventual tomorrow. We do know this much, and it's enough. Jesus is "the firstborn from the dead (Col 1:18). We who belong to Christ will be next in line for our rebirths (1 Cor 15:23). "Thanks be to God who gives us the victory through our Lord Jesus Christ (1 Cor 15:57).

A major part of the good news is that the resurrection victory that lies ahead already is at work in those who are in Christ (Eph 1:19–20).[152] "Return to us, O God Almighty! Care for what you once tenderly planted" (Ps 80:14–18 *The Message*).

We must be prepared for things more marvelous than any of our expectations. What's soon to arrive will stretch our imaginations, shatter our limited categories, and go beyond what our feeble words now are able to express. Paul says this. "So here I am, preaching and writing about things that are way over my head, the inexhaustible riches and generosity of Christ" (Eph 3:8).

The Bible refers to the sea as the dreaded chaos over which humans have no control (Matt 8:2-27; Acts 27:13-41). Nothing, however, is beyond God's control and all believers are headed back to God where there will be *no more sea* (Rev 21:1).

> Come, let us join our friends above who have obtained the prize, and on the eagle wings of love to joys celestial rise.[153]

****

Jesus with the Final Word

(in part a paraphrase of Luke 6:20-31, Col 1:11-20)

Know at least this, my friends, about your final home. I'm building it for you. Since I love you so much, it will be really something! The critical thing for you to know now is how to get there. Dr. Luke's presentation of my "Sermon on the Plain," as people sometimes call it, gives you my vivid picture of life as it should be lived under the reign of my Father while on your way to your new home.

To be pitied are those who are self-satisfied, at ease in their wealth, happily gaining from the present order of things, filling their pockets on the backs of the poor. To arrive home later, you must learn the loving art of giving away now. I know selfless love isn't always a comfortable way to exist. They hung me. It's just my way, and the only way for you.

My Father sent me to pay every price needed in order that you might live forever alongside the Ever-living One. My Father has taken the initiative to restore and soon resurrect you to new life and being with him at home forever. He has liberated humankind from the grip of darkness and granted an inheritance of light to all the saints. You can be among them. Amazing! See you there! I go now to get all things ready.

32

WHO WILL BE IN HEAVEN? SURPRISE!

We believers tend to separate in our minds those, at least in our judgment, who are heaven bound and those who are not. If being eternally saved requires accepting Jesus as the one and only Savior, then we're quite sure we can spot those on their way up and those headed down. Heaven will be filled with the people who believed as we do and maybe even looked much like we look.

We, however, will not be the One at heaven's gate sorting the arrivals and announcing either "Welcome Home!" or "I Never Knew You!" God created all people, loves all people, and surely has issued all people an opportunity to walk the ways that lead to life eternal. The Judge will review the life limitations and decisions made by each arrival. Could it be that some will be admitted who never even heard of Jesus? I'm glad I'm not that Judge!

Heaven is pictured in Revelation 21 as a communal celebration of all God's people from all times and places. The numerous saints of God will be there together, rejoicing, worshipping around God's throne, and eating at his lavish banquet table. All evil will have ended and righteousness and justice finally will have prevailed.

Population Uncertainty

One big remaining question is this. Who will be in this great number? Who are the saints saved for eternity? When the Book of Life is opened, how long and diverse will be the list of names? Christians annually celebrate "All Saints Day." With whom are we celebrating on that day?

The population of this world is large and quite diverse. Will it be the same in heaven? What about the biblical claim of "Jesus only" as the exclusive way to get in? Jesus did say, "I am *the* way and *the* truth and *the* life. No one comes to the Father except through me" (Jn 14:6). This dramatic claim views the revelation of God to ancient Israel and then finally in Jesus Christ as the fully adequate and only route into heaven for all the world's people across all its history.

Seemingly implied is that this single way must be consciously known and embraced by an individual if there is hope of eternal salvation. This exclusiveness sometimes is called the "scandal" of Christianity. Exactly what did Jesus mean? Doesn't this Jesus-only particularity unfairly limit heaven's population? After all, the majority of humanity has lived and died without ever hearing the Christian gospel. That includes everyone before Jesus was on earth and more billions after. Are these people automatically excluded from heaven merely by their ignorance of the name Jesus, no fault of their own?

What's the proper Christian attitude toward non-Jesus people, especially those who never heard the name but nonetheless were (are) serious about what they believe and how they live? Does God's redeeming love transcend the walls of human ignorance and the church's success at evangelizing? What about Christian churches and their members who carry the Jesus name but have very faulty theological thinking if any at all? Does the most shallow claiming of belonging to Jesus count in the end? I rejoice at not having to be the final judge!

God's Gracious Spirit Is Universal

We know at least this much from biblical revelation. The people who will get into heaven will share one thing. They all will be sinners who have received the forgiving love of God and placed their faith in the Lord Jesus Christ (Jn 1:12; Acts 16:31; Rom 10:9). The Bible takes sin seriously and doesn't encourage us to think that everyone will accept God's love, although offered to all.

Nor are we encouraged by the Bible to believe that God will use superior power to eventually overcome all of love's rejections. "Universalists" are convinced that the love of God is so great that eventually all persons will be won to it, even it takes some severe discipline after death. This is a lovely thought that likely is more idealism that realism. We see in the ministry of Jesus a reluctance to force anyone to believe. Our freedom of choice is real and has eternal consequences.

The Bible does emphasize the universality of Christ's atonement. He died for all sinners and "the ever-present Spirit can enable transforming relationships with God anywhere and everywhere. This inspires hope for our personal futures and for the future of the world, including the many ungodly whom God clearly wishes to justify" (Rom 15:13).[154] Paul emphasizes what God has done *for us*, not what we have accomplished *for him*.

Salvation rests not our great accomplishments in life but on how much God loves us in Jesus Christ. It's less what we've *done* in our weakness and ignorance and much more what we've gratefully *received* by grace from a loving God. This seems to leave the door of hope open a little for anyone who has ever lived. I accept the biblical declaration that Christ is the only Mediator between God and humans. I also accept another biblical teaching. Biblical truth often comes in paradoxes.

The Spirit of God, who pre-dates and post-dates the Christ atonement that occurred at one point in our human history (the cross of Jesus), offers hope for salvation beyond direct engagement with that historical event. It surely is possible, given the great love of God, to have cast oneself on the mercy of God even if born long before Jesus first appeared as a baby in Bethlehem.

God can create sons and daughters of Abraham as God chooses, even if they never had opportunity to hear of the Old and New Testaments. The true children of Abraham are those of true faith (Gal 3:7). Can faith be meaningful for salvation even if poorly informed about Gpd's historical actions? How many Christians do you know who seem to know little more about biblical contents than the average non-believer on the streets? Will they be held responsible for the knowledge so readily available to them?

God is the divine "Person" and all human persons can receive the gift of divine love. Person-to-person is the arena of God's saving ministry through the Spirit of God. This saving can happen without the person knowing the name of divine giver, exactly how much the salvation cost, or when and how it was paid. It's important to be aware of one big element of Christian theology.

Grace Provides Opportunity

"Prevenient grace" is a critical biblical teaching. It refers to the gracious and universal ministry of the Spirit of God who comes to all persons *before* any human deserving or ability to respond.[155] This coming provides at least minimal awareness of divine love and the ability to respond in faith to God's satisfaction. The Spirit is working savingly everywhere. People universally are enabled by the Spirit to open themselves humbly to the loving work of Jesus even if not knowing his name or his redemptive work on the cross.

The Spirit enables all persons to become candidates for a personal address somewhere in heaven. One thief on a cross next to Jesus became at least vaguely aware of what Jesus was about and asked to be part of the future of his kingdom. Jesus said he would be a part even though he qualified in no way other than his expressed desire based on virtually no information about Judaism or the work of Jesus. The man only knew that whoever Jesus was must be who God is.

A basic knowledge of God is universally available. Such knowledge is the Spirit's extension of God's gracious and sacrificial activity in Jesus Christ. The cross of Jesus was in the heart of God before it was planted in a hill outside Jerusalem. Otherwise, it never would have appeared on our historical scene.[156] The reaching and saving love of God was active before, during, and after the actual cross event in Israel. Jesus existed long before the man from Nazareth was in our human midst (Jn 1). This implies that what happened in and around Jerusalem is embedded without Hebrew names in the searching of honest souls worldwide.

Anyone can benefit from God having been with us in Jesus, and apart from any direct awareness of the name Jesus or his historical life and saving work. All human response to the love of God in Christ is possible only because of the enlightening presence of God's grace. That grace, always is rooted in the atoning work of

Christ, has been and continues to be savingly active in the universal ministry of Christ's Spirit.

The Wesleyan-Holiness tradition of Christianity stresses the importance of human response to divine grace. It hesitates to embrace "universalism" (all persons finally will be saved). God reaches to all, although likely all will not respond in faith and be "saved." Confidence in the central role God in Jesus always is warranted. Even so, a claim to knowing precisely heaven's eventual numbers, ethnicities, denominations, faith communities, and theological understandings *is not*.

Errors to Avoid

There are two errors that apparently should be avoided given the biblical revelation. One is saying dogmatically that all people eventually will be saved. If they resist God's saving love, eventually that love will yield sadly to God's judgment on sin. The other is saying dogmatically that only a select few will be saved, God having decided in advance the final population of heaven.

We what we should do is focus on the wonder of the amazing grace of God and spread the good news of Christ as widely as possible. Having done that, we are to leave the rest to God's work and final wisdom.

There are brief references in the New Testament to God's "predestination." This much can be said. The creating God originally intended there to be no sin. Humanity fell into sin by its own choice and now there will be consequences. God's clear intention is that all people be redeemed if all will respond in gratitude and faithfulness. Those who do respond are predestined *in Christ* to an eternal home above. All individuals are predestined who by choice come to be and choose to remain *in Christ*.

There are sordid instances in church history when a ruler and conquering army forced whole populations to become "Christian" (at least in name). The love of God, however, is not coercive like that and such politically motivated identity switching is hardly an instant ticket to heaven. Human response in faith to the reaching of divine love is necessary. While there is room in heaven for all people, many will choose not to accept the invitation. Those who persist in their fallenness will leave vacant their provided heavenly places.

Death is the moment of our return to God. It's the end of the faith journey, the culmination of our response to God's great love offer. It's the fulfillment of the eternal life we've already begun to live in our union with Christ or the closing of the offered opportunity to be in such a divine union. God calls us to our place of choice. "Eternity can be within our hearts now, calling us home to itself."[157] It also can be rejected now, altering our track forever away from our home.

****

Jesus with the Final Word

There are many references to "all peoples" in the Bible. My Father's redemptive work through me has universal intent and now, through my Spirit, universal impact. The divine light shines on all. All are invited to the great banquet feast of eternity. Many will not come, unfortunately. All will choose whether or not to be in me throughout eternity. All will be judged by my Father. The judgment will be fair and final. Don't pre-judge, my friends, just witness with joy and trust my Father.

Relate lovingly to all people, partly because some of them, to your great surprise, may later be joining you in heaven! "About that day and hour no one knows, only the Father. Be alert at all times. All authority in heaven and on earth has been given to me. Go therefore and make disciples of *all nations*" (Matt 24:36; Lk 21:36; Matt 28:18-19). As you go, gladly sing the following inspired words, leaving to me and my Father decisions about who will be included in "all the servants of our King."

> Let saints on earth unite, to sing with those to glory gone,
> for all the servants of our King, in earth and heaven are one.[158]

33

THE WAY TO WAIT? ACTIVATE!

Sitting out the present troubled times, waiting for the perfect set of circumstances to arrive, is an unacceptable life stance for disciples of Jesus. The idealized time will never come. Christian holiness is love in action *now*. God's promises are sure in relation to tomorrow. What about today before those promises are fulfilled?

While Jesus will return and one day justice will be done, remember this. Jesus already *has come*. The clear call is to be on God's mission now! True saints of the Master are filled with the already present Spirit who goes and serves and beckons us to go as present agents of love. The harvest fields are ripe and waiting for our harvesting.[159] Tomorrow could be too late. Don't just wait. Activate!

Faith traveling for Christians involves two things, both required. One is to hold steady, the other to move ahead. We must know and remain where we are as we plan where and how to go. Any GPS wants to know present location and intended destination. Disciples of Jesus are to be and to be on the way.

Still and In Motion

An Italian travel guide reports a lovely habit many have in her country. On a clear night people lie on the grass in front of their homes and gaze at the Milky Way in the distant sky. The sparkling stars help them realize something important. True life involves opposing thoughts that together form a grand truth. Here they are.

It's important to be on solid ground; it's equally important to realize that the very ground beneath you is itself in rapid motion as the planet circles the sun. Life needs to be rooted firmly and enroute daily. We Christians are pilgrims who need to know for sure where we are and that we are to be on the way to the proper elsewhere.

We function in the stillness of the present while focusing on our motion into the future. We know and don't know. We are home and still on the way. Anyone who hopes to reign with Christ in heaven must have Christ reigning within on earth. Getting to our ultimate home means going there in all our present times. The best waiting is active preparation for immediate activating!

As we lie in the grass and gaze into the night sky, every breath we take is an opportunity to shape a path that travels on behalf of the eternities. In a sense, we humans begin at the end because we live from that for which we hope. We act now from what we desire and because of who we love.[160] It's the Spirit of God who makes present and real the resurrected and living Christ. Our hope in him requires immediate mission now. The call is to be stable, rooted, full of faith, and inspired by this hope to be actively on the way.

The Pentecost Plan

The biblical story of Pentecost is about the Spirit of Christ coming *to* us in order to be *in* us (experienced holiness). Why in us? So that God may move *through* us as redeeming love addressing a broken world (expressed holiness). Let's avoid the fruitless process of future speculation and focus on the demands of present proclamation. The Spirit of Jesus is here to make all the difference in what we can be and what's to be done prior to our final arrival home.

The Christian community was launched initially at Pentecost by vigorous preaching about the bursting forth of a new age in the "last days." The first Christian evangelists were sure they knew what time it was in God's eyes. It was the fullness of time, the beginning of the end, the present arrival of the divine reign in the coming of Jesus. They were being sent out to the whole world with great news.

It had taken the resurrection of Jesus for them to realize that what they had seen on that terrible cross was not the triumph of this world's power. It was an unexpected presentation of the amazing power of the love of the Father for all of lost humankind. We now know who holds the future. We now know what constitutes the very heart of the Eternal. It's love for us and all others.

As loyal disciples blessed with such knowledge, we must do as the Italians are said to do. We must rest in this amazing truth and then go forth from it and with it on behalf of all others. Gaze into the starry skies and know that the whole earth is in motion as we now are to be.

A classic poem is *"The Negro Speaks of Rivers."* A humble man had stretched out in the grass and gazed into the clear night sky. "My soul has grown deep like the rivers."[161] He had seen and found his own identity and mission by glimpsing into the depths of things. When the end of life comes, he and I and hopefully you will want to have lived not only life's full length, but also its entire width, height, and depth. We want to have felt solid ground and soared into the skies with the Spirit. We want to have been still and in motion.

The New Testament teaching about the "resurrection of the body" means at least that in the coming life beyond we again will be ourselves. Of course, all will be possible because God still will be God! How we then will be "packaged" as persons doesn't matter and is beyond our present knowing.

"My soul longs, indeed it faints for the courts of the Lord; my heart and my flesh sing for joy to the living God" (Ps 84:1-2). Meanwhile, we are to be active, fruitful in our waiting. We should long for the will of God to be done *on earth* as one day it will be *in heaven*. Wait and activate! Later there will come the time to sing and dance.

Paul reassured the Philippians that the God "who began a good work in you will carry it on to completion" (Phil 1:6). One day all will be eternal light. What then are we to do while the divine sunrise is still delayed? According to Paul, "the night is about over, morning is about to break. Be up and awake doing your part in assisting what God is doing. God is putting the finishing touches on the salvation work he began when we first believed" (Rom 13:12).

Just a Glimpse Ahead

We children of God are to be activating our gifts of the Spirit as partners in the ongoing divine work. The coming kingdom of love already is established in the hearts and lives and communities of those who now mirror the love of Christ through acts of compassion and cries for justice.[162] Given this activated reality, here's a glimpse of the coming final conclusion.

"Then comes the end when Christ hands over the kingdom to God the Father after he has destroyed every ruler and authority and power. For he must reign until he has put all enemies under his feet" (1 Cor 15:24-25). Are you discouraged? Look up, keep gazing into the night sky, feel the solid ground beneath, know that things are in motion toward the proper end. Move on in faith! Why the excitement? "For the Lord our God Almighty reigns!" (Rev 19:6).

The people of God are to know themselves better by looking at the moon of divine destiny through the telescope of God's revelation. We then see that we are saints called to refract this moonlight, causing it to shine on others.[163] God's Spirit is the shining power of life that makes us really alive.

In this experience of new life, we redeemed humans come close to the origin and reason for all things. The power of this fresh life is the power of the future world. New life in Christ kindles the beginning of the process that reaches beyond death.[164] If the church abides in God, God will dependably abide in the church (Jn 15:4).

As we gaze upward into the night skies, one truth must grasp us tightly and send us forward excitedly. Jesus Christ is the all-sufficiency of life for us who believe. Provided in Jesus are all the hidden treasures of wisdom and knowledge (Col 2:3). Jesus alone is necessary and sufficient for our salvation (Col 1:14).

Christian is to be infused with thanksgiving for this magnificent truth. Jesus Christ is the visible expression of the invisible God, the Alpha and Omega (Rev 22:13), the full alphabet of past, present, and future reality (Col 1:15-18). Nothing greater can be conceived and nothing less is adequate for Christian belief and life.

The amazing reality of Jesus Christ gives our identity as disciples solid rootage as we proceed in this world. It puts us on the sure path that is known to be on its way to the skies of all eternity. God's grace is fresh every day. May we fix our eyes on that wonderful reality! May we always keep moving, activating, hoping, and singing as we go . . .

Thou, who's purpose is to kindle, now ignite us with Thy fire;
While the earth awaits Thy burning, with Thy passion us inspire.
Overcome our sinful calmness, rouse us with redemptive shame;
Baptize with Thy fiery Spirit, crown our lives with tongues of flame.[165]

****

Jesus with the Final Word

(in part a paraphrase of Mark 8:27-38)

My dear friends, your calling as my disciples demands a high level of sensitivity to the guidance of my Spirit. That sensitivity must be nurtured regularly by an intentional waiting, a gazing upward and denying of yourselves. It must feature the carrying of your individual crosses of self-sacrifice as you follow me. Staying close enables you to know who I really am and who you are supposed to become. Remember that just ahead you will encounter your own joyous Easters. The big question isn't who the public thinks I am but who *you* think I am. Know me, follow me, and you will come to know who my Father intends and will enable you to be.

If you lose your life for my sake and activate the good news I bring, you will be saved eternally (Mk 8:35). My church wishes all the questions were answered in advance. Since that's not the case, you believers must be fully committed to me, your common Lord, and actively pursue unity and mission with each other regardless of your lack of knowledge and many differences. Let me leave you with crucial guiding wisdom.

Above all, when my Spirit speaks to you, be sure you really hear and put into practice whatever is said. Never forget that I am the Father's very Word of life come to you in human form. Keep close to me and to your sisters and brothers in the faith so that together you may be able to reflect to the world my redemptive and healing love. Be open and flexible as new days arrive. Know that the church's yesterday does not necessarily determine everything about its tomorrows. First wait, then activate!

We now have asked many of our pressing questions about the Christian faith. How wonderful that God listens patiently to our many concerns. However, now we must stop asking! Finally, God speaks, asking us four critical questions. These put everything into divine perspective. It's time to listen to God and respond appropriately. God always should be given the last questions!

34

GOD'S QUESTION: "WHO DO YOU THINK I AM?" OUR RESPONSE: "HELP ME KNOW, LORD!"

God is bigger than we usually or ever can think. Our human thinking isn't capable of comprehending the totality of God. When we use only our limited means of measuring, we won't ever be able to manage life successfully with its sufferings and divine callings. Neither could Job. He was in big trouble and his best friends had done their frustrating best to help him understand.

Then came the voice of God. He had tired of the flow of demanding questions shot his way. Job had talked long enough and was so wrong in assuming that God wasn't paying attention or at least had nothing to say.

Job wouldn't back down and God thundered back with a flurry of his own questions that rendered the suffering and confused man stunned and silent. The first question was, "Who do you think I am? And, Job, who do you think you are?" When God answers, our human questions just melt into the background (Job 38-40).

"Pull yourself together, Job. Why are you talking so much about what you don't understand in the slightest? You don't seem to know who I really am. Be quiet now because I have some questions for you, and I expect some straight answers if you have them. Ready?"

"Where were you when I created the earth? Who drew the blueprints? Who took charge of the ocean when it gushed forth like a baby from the womb? That was me! I wrapped it in soft clouds and tucked it in safely for the night. By the way, Job, have you ever ordered the morning to get up and the dawn to again do its lovely work? I do it every day."

"Do you have a clue about death's dark mysteries or where light comes from so you can lead them home if they should ever get lost? Can you find your way to where lightening is launched or hail is stockpiled? How then do you presume to tell me what I'm doing wrong? Are you calling me a thoughtless sinner so you can think of yourself as a soaring saint? Can you save yourself with no help from me? I urge you not to try!" Job was now completely silent and the Voice from above continued.

"Hear this, Job. 'Thus saith the LORD, the King of Israel, and Israel's Redeemer, the LORD of hosts. I am the first and the last and beside me there is no God' (Isa 44:6). Hear my voice thunder from the throne. 'Look! God has moved into the neighborhood, making his home with men and women. They're my people, I'm their God. I'll wipe every tear from their eyes. Death will be gone for good-- tears gone, crying gone, pain gone, making everything new. Write down each word, dependable and accurate'" (Rev 2:3-5). Then came some final divine words.

"Job, beyond your time people will come to know clearly what I'm telling you now. The strength needed to endure the injustices of the present will be graciously discovered in my Son Jesus and conveyed to creatures like you through my Spirit. The One who will die and yet lives forevermore will invite all people to be made strong with all the strength that comes from this glorious power (Col 1:11). The power reigning over heaven and earth is the power of *love*. It will be demonstrated dramatically in the life, death, and resurrection of Rabbi Jesus, in whom all the fullness of Myself will be pleased to dwell" (Col 1:19).

God had these and more questions and declarations for Job, who now was just staring in silence and seemed to have no more questions. We humans often don't understand the flow of human events and raise urgent and yet lame questions for God. God finally says that some answers are quite beyond us while we wander through our very limited human times. We must relax, have faith, move on, and keep an eye out for the coming Jesus.

Rather than demanding answers, some of which might not now be within our human reach, we should be humbled at the greatness of God and believe that one day, somehow, somewhere, it all will become clear. Meanwhile, we are to be living in faith above the questions and beyond the doubts.

God expects a humble answer from us. **"Who do you think I am?"**

35

GOD'S QUESTION: "WHAT ARE YOU DOING THERE?" OUR RESPONSE: "I'M HIDING"

God finds us wherever we are, and often it's in a bad place that's hardly God's plan for our present lives. God sees us faltering and understands our plight more clearly than we can understand ourselves. God shows up behind our self-protective masks, knows our temptation to give up, and says this to Elijah who was on the run.

"You're in a cave hiding? Why? I know the depressing story of how you got there. Still, you tell me anyway, Elijah. You need to hear yourself talking and see the bigger picture far better than you do now. Things need to change and you need to get out of there, and soon. Take off that mask. Stand tall because you are my ambassador. I'm here to help."

"Are you listening, Elijah? Are you willing? Can you dare to be real and get back in the game? Important things are waiting for you elsewhere. Know me and you will know yourself better and why you still are urgently needed in my great cause."

The word of the Lord came to Elijah (1 Kings 19). "Elijah, what are you doing in there?" The scared man answers awkwardly.

"I've been working my heart out for you, God. It's no good. The Israelites have rejected your covenant, torn down your altars, and put your prophets to death with the sword. I am the only one left, and now they are trying to kill me too! I'm trying to escape to some safety and maybe die on my own. That's why I'm in this stupid cave!"

"OK, Elijah, I hear you. You really need to listen up. You are to go back where you came from and dare to act there as I'll now explain. Once you've heard the details, get out of that cave and go. Granted, you won't know everything in advance or always be safe, but at least you'll know the first steps to take and who you really are. There are many souls who haven't given up on our great work, whether you know it or not, and you've got to join them again. Don't forget the wonderful things I've done in the past. I assure you that more good is on the way and you are still very much in the picture. Let's go!"

That was then, this is now. Did you ever think you have done your best, things haven't worked out, and now you're depressed or worse, trying to hide just to survive, or maybe even hurt yourself? Yesterday was a bust and you can barely handle today. Tomorrow may be only a sad fiction to be avoided if possible. If this is your situation, Elijah is your biblical man. What a mess he was in. He had run away and was hoping to end it all. Then came that small voice of the Great One who had a much clearer view of yesterday, today, and tomorrow.

Elijah's life was filled with turmoil. At times he was bold and decisive and at other times fearful and tentative. He alternately demonstrated victory and defeat. This battle-weary prophet knew both the power of God and the depths of depression. Here's the confession of a modern Christian disciple with a troubled personal history and an important message:

> God asks us not to hide in shame but to bring all our "stuff" to him, all the dirty laundry we carry on our own backs. And with a great gesture of gentleness, God asks if he can have it. He wants to bring his love to our brokenness and his holiness to our humanity.[166]

God is looking for honesty that dares to face the worst head-on. Elijah managed at least the first step. He spelled out the real situation as he was experiencing it. He acknowledged that he was existing in fear, not faith, and had taken his eyes off the Lord and locked them on his disturbing circumstances. According to God, he needed the following lesson.

The Christian Negro spirituals are songs in the night. They are shafts of light and often documents of social protest. They are outcries of longing for needed change. They have a persistent perspective regarding God. It's a profound conviction that no problems or human masters have the last word where faith reigns. God is and God rules, God sends and God provides, regardless. This is the music of searchers who had found something eternal and Someone immortal.[167]

The titles of these spirituals say it all on God's behalf. "Sometimes I Feel Like a Motherless Child!" "Nobody Knows the Trouble I've Seen." "Didn't My Lord Deliver Daniel?" "Take My Hand, Precious Lord."

God is asking us: **"What are you doing there?"**

36

GOD'S QUESTION: "WHAT'S THAT IN YOUR HAND?" OUR RESPONSE: "JUST A STAFF"

God has big plans for changes in this broken world and keeps calling faithful ones to assist with means he will enable. Often we think we have nothing left, no way to engage in a righteous battle. Our best efforts so far have been undermined by the faithlessness of others. What's the point of trying to go on? That takes us from Elijah in a cave to Moses in the desert. Both were cornered and yet sent. We all are disciples in the making.

God cornered Moses by surprise and proposed a huge mission for him to lead. The poor man panicked, thinking of himself as nobody in the face of what God had in mind.

> Moses: "I just can't and so I won't!"
> God: "Moses, what's that in your hand?"
> Moses: "Nothing much, just a stick I use with the sheep."
> God: "Then let's start there. You need a much bigger vision
> of who you might be if you would only go in my
> name and do as I say. When I'm with you, you
> can be my amazing somebody, regardless of the past!
> Let's talk about that stick."

God came and shocked Moses in the desert (Ex 3-4). The lonely shepherd saw or thought he saw a bush flaming brightly but not being consumed. People sometimes think they see strange things in the desert that just aren't there.

"Take off your shoes, Moses, you are standing on holy ground! I am God."

Was that voice real? Was the poor man going mad in the sun? Moses was afraid and God went on talking.

"I've taken a good look at the injustice being suffered by my people in Egypt. It's time for a big change and I've chosen you to take the lead. My people are to be brought out to freedom and I'm about to send you to Pharaoh to have him let them go from their awful slavery."

How does one experience sunstroke, or was this really a God-stroke?

"Excuse me, God, if that's really you, but I'm nobody and Pharaoh runs that Egyptian world like he's the real God. You've surely got the wrong man. Why would anyone ever listen if I spoke to Egyptian royalty?"

"Good question, Moses. The short answer is because I will be with you and the ultimate speaking will be mine."

"I think I need the long answer, God! Who would I tell the Israelites had sent me with this dramatic message? At least give me your name."

"No problem. Tell them you were sent by *'I-AM-WHO-I-AM.'* This is the name above all names, the One who just is and was with their fathers and now will be with my people as they hear and heed your words. Go to them and to Pharaoh and tell them who I am and what I want. I want my people out of there!"

"But, *I-AM-WHO-I-AM*, that would be like me turning the whole world upside down. It would never work, and I have plenty of reason to know. For the first forty years of my life I lived as a member of Pharaoh's household. When I became aware of your peoples' oppression, I exacted some vigilante justice on an oppressive Egyptian man and had to flee for my life. That's how I ended up here tending sheep in the isolated fields of Midian. I'm hiding, a man on the run. I know Egypt well, I'm especially unwelcome there, and I don't want to go back—ever! So aren't you sure you're not kidding?"

"It would be *Me* doing the turning, Moses, certainly not you. I've got the right man and when I'm done Pharaoh will be glad to let my people go. Maybe this will help you. Let me quote what my man

Paul will write many generations from now: 'What is foolish in the world will shame the wise and strong so that no human being might boast in the presence of God' (1 Cor 1:26-29).' By the way, Moses, what's that in your hand?"

"A simple staff to work with the sheep. It's just a stick like me."

"Throw it on the ground." Moses did and had to jump back because it now was a deadly snake!

"Pick it up!" Moses cautiously reached for the tail hoping not to die from an awful bite, but it again was just a stick in his hand. Maybe he *was* dealing with God. Even so, all he could think of were excuses for staying where he was or running back to the sheep, pretending that these bush and snake things had never happened.

"God, I can't make speeches to the king of the whole Egyptian world. Sometimes even sheep won't listen to me."

"Enough talk, Moses. It's travel time. Are you coming?"

The point Moses was missing was that it was God addressing him, and God can use even injured and timid people as long as they look to the Lord for wisdom and strength. It's not human ability but *availability* that's being requested. We humans may have very, very little in our hands. Maybe that's just how God prefers it. Little is much when God is in it. A staff or whatever will do just fine. Get ready Egypt. Moses is coming!

God is asking us, **"What's that in your hand?"**

37

GOD'S QUESTION: "WHOM THEN SHALL I SEND?" OUR RESPONSE: "SEND ME!"

We limited humans often find ourselves failing to understand by faith who God really is. That leaves us hiding in depression, doubtful that we have anything much to offer, and maybe have no future at all. Surely God no longer is planning exceptional things to happen through us frail nobodies. We must deal with the haunting question Jesus once posed to his disciples. "Will you come and follow me and then go in my Spirit to a waiting world?"

The classic example is the prophet Isaiah. He once was a broken sinner and became responsible for some amazing biblical writing that Jesus seemed to know by heart and often quoted while here on earth. This mere man once heard the voice of the Lord saying directly to him, "Whom shall I send and who will go for us?" Isaiah wasn't inclined positively at first, and then he was.

There came to Isaiah an awareness of God, a humble repentance, cleansing coals of fire, and then this surprising declaration. "Send me!" (Isa 6:1-8). When he (we) know who God really is (Job), become willing to leave our current hiding place (Elijah), and recognize that a simple staff in our hands can become an effective instrument of God (Moses), then it's time to go!

It was in the year that King Uzziah died, but that's not important. It could be anytime, even right now. What's important is that Isaiah saw a vision of the heavenly throne and heard the voice of God calling him personally. Life changed. Divine mission engagement required seeing a vision of the Lord who ignites within a response of "holy, holy, holy!" That stuns one with an awareness that this God is not anxious to condemn our sinfulness but rather cleanse it with the hot coals of undeserved love.

Isaiah saw, realized, repented, and was graciously cleansed. Then what? Then came a question from God. "I need a prophet just like you, Isaiah. Will you go for me?"

Isaiah's grateful response was, "I hear you, Lord, I love you and, if you will go with me, I will go wherever you direct!" God's response was, "You got it, my good man. You'll never be alone, although the people you will address for me often will not respond well in their blindness and selfishness. No matter. Let's go—together!"

One day Jesus, who appeared to know Isaiah's later writings by heart, would urge us all to such repentance and commitment (Lk 8:26-39). "My Father is the great lover who seeks to pour love and mission into all of you. You must form churches that offer gracious spaces where the wounded and isolated can come to be heard and restored. My Father reaches out with cleansing coals to enable restored relationships. Why? Because of a great love. Your mission, should you accept, is to show and tell that love to all people you can."

That's exactly what God had called Isaiah to do. The restoring grace of the loving Father reaches beyond every barrier that human sin and society build. God is relational love in action, always reaching and restoring. We are to learn to reach out lovingly to others as part of our Father's work. Now, like to Isaiah, God is saying, "I send *you*." Our response is to be, "Yes, Lord, I'm ready to go if you will go with me!"

Job, Elijah, Moses, Isaiah, and now you and I are all faced with the same questions from God. Will we go as God directs, doing as God says, knowing by faith that the mission is possible? The possibility is not because of who we are but because of *who God is*. The promise always is this. "I will be with you!"

Prince Caspian is a featured character in the *Chronicles of Narnia* by C. S. Lewis. After the decisive battle, Aslan, the great Lion, reports surprisingly that the Prince now was able to assume his rightful kingship. But Caspian remained uncertain about his readiness for such a large responsibility. He was grateful but humble. Aslan then offers this telling judgment. "It's for that very reason that I know you are ready!" Humility is a clear mark of Christian maturity, a holy readiness for major responsibility.

I shared this toward the conclusion of my autobiography.[168] My wife and I had just watched a TV documentary about the lives and careers of our friends Bill and Gloria Gaither. They lived close to our home in central Indiana and had been named "Songwriters of the Twentieth Century" in the field of Christian music, composers of beloved songs like "He Touched Me," "Because He Lives," "The King Is Coming," and many more. The documentary showed how this gifted Christian couple had taken the "old" and made it work in fresh ways for new times.

Here's the lesson, the biblical challenge, the best way to go about life, the right way to respond to God's questions and call. You and I can choose to look back and lament the wonderful things once known and now gone or at least changed almost beyond recognition. Or we can look back and rejoice in past privileges that were ours and focus on the wisdom gained from yesterday's struggles.

Such rejoicing and focusing will draw from yesterday the strength and wisdom necessary for handling wisely the present, and for joining God who says it's time to move on to a new future. The fortunate truth is that we Christian people on mission are not called to be *successful*, only *faithful*. Success rests on the larger shoulders of God. God asks the biggest questions and responds with the only adequate answers.

We disciples of Jesus sometimes must go forward with unanswered questions, coming out of the caves where we are hiding, even from ourselves, out of the deserts with only little staffs in our hands, but with the cleansing coals of love in our hearts and on our lips. Most of all, we can be enabled to face the future knowing who God really is and that God walks by our sides. That's enough. Let's go!!

God calls and equips even you and me. **"Whom then shall I send?"**

A POSTSCRIPT OF ENCOURAGEMENT

I have posed many difficult questions. Are they now answered? Yes, partly, mostly, but not fully. We Christians are pilgrims seeing only in part and learning more only as we go much farther along in our faith journeys. In the meantime, the needed guidance is presented well in one of the great New Testament chapters, Hebrews eleven.

A multitude of believers have gone before us and managed by faith. The biblical writer presents a long list of such people, times, and issues. There is so much left unresolved for the church until journey's end. How did all these believers make it with many of their pressing questions still unanswered and their tough issues not yet resolved? *By faith!*

Here's the simple secret. When following the all-knowing Shepherd, there's no need to be all-knowing yourself. Just trust and keep following as closely as possible. Knowledge will increase along the way. One day we will know even as we now are known.

Did the faithful disciples of yesterday get anything done while still in this vale of tears? According to Hebrews eleven, "They toppled kingdoms, made justice work, took the promises for themselves. They were protected, turned disadvantage to advantage, and routed alien armies. They made their way as best they could on the cruel edges of the world they knew."

Not one of these persons of faith was fully satisfied, totally successful, without fault or failure. Even so, with some promises yet unfulfilled and questions yet unanswered, they all became spiritually whole, satisfactorily accomplished God's will, and eventually found their way home.

The good Shepherd always can be trusted. Keep believing. Follow closely. Keep moving. It's all light up ahead!

We all learn by standing on the shoulders of others and asking questions. I have done this throughout this book without burdening you with the details. Even so, you may wish to follow up on something by going to the original sources that informed me. Thus, there now appears the list of my Endnotes. They are paths to sources of additionl Christian wisdom.

ENDNOTES

1 See Stephen N. Finlan, *The Drama of Job: Burning Questions and Incomplete Answers*, 2025.

2 Verse one of Eliza E. Hewitt's hymn "More About Jesus Would I Know."

3 Eric Weiner, *The Socrates Express*, 2020.

4 See chapter one of this biblical book, especially in *The Message* paraphrase.

5 The film is *Dead Poets Society*, 1989.

6 Brenna Blain, *Can I Say That?*, 2024.

7 Gloria Gaither, personal blog of December 6, 2024.

8 *"Who Will Answer"* by Sheila Davis and others, sung by Ed Ames and others.

9 Brenna Blain, *Can I Say That?*, 2024.

10 David Liverett, editor and illustrator, *Questions for God*, 2009.

11 Winn Collier, *A Burning in My Bones*, the biography of Eugene H. Peterson, 2021.

12 D. Elton Trueblood, *Philosophy of Religion*, 1951.

13 Bishop Kallistos Ware, *The Orthodox Way*.

14 Walter Brueggemann, *Finally Comes the Poet*.

15 Barry L. Callen, *The Living Dead*.

16 These testimonies are by Blaise Pascal and David Elton Trueblood.

17 This was the testimony of Dr. Gene W. Newberry offered to Barry L. Callen.

18 If you wish considerable detail, see Barry L. Callen, *Discerning the Divine*.

19 William Willimon, *Proclamation and Theology*.

20 Dennis F. Kinlaw, *Lectures in Old Testament Theology*.

21 Marvin Wilson, *Our Father Abraham*.

22 William Kent Krueger, *This Tender Land*.

23 See Barry Callen, *The Jagged Journey*.

24 Clark H. Pinnock in the *Wesleyan Theological Journal*, Fall, 2003.

25 Clark Pinnock, *Flame of Love*.

26 Gregory Boyd, *God of the Possible*.

27 Clark H. Pinnock, *Most Moved Mover*.

28 For a quality commentary on this ancient Christian creed, see Jerome Van Kuiken, *The Creed We Need*.

29 Barry L. Callen, *Bible Stories for Strong Stomachs*.

30 Clark H. Pinnock, *The Most Moved Mover*.

31 Barry L. Callen, *God As Loving Grace* and Clark H. Pinnock, *Flame of Love*.

32 Barry L. Callen, *Discerning the Divine*, and *Heart of the Matter*.

33 Words of Quaker philosopher David Elton Trueblood in his Foreword to Barry L. Callen, *Caught Between Truths*.

34 Alfred North Whitehead, *Science and the Modern World*.

35 From the poem "*A Lost Chord*" by Adelaide Anne Procter.

36 Barry L. Callen, *Caught Between Truths*, especially chapter one.

37 Barry L. Callen, *Bible Stories for Strong Stomachs*.

38 Hubert Harriman and Barry Callen, *Color Me Holy*.

39 Excerpt from the hymn "*Lead On, O King Eternal*" by Ernest Shurtleff.

40 Elie Wiesel, *Night*.

41 C. S. Lewis, *Mere Christianity*. Also, William Temple, *Nature, Man, and God*, and David Elton Trueblood, *The Logic of Belief*.

42 Barry L. Callen, *The Jagged Journey*.

43 Don Thorsen, *What's True about Christianity?*

44 Jürgen Moltmann, *The Living God and the Fullness of Life*.

45 D. Elton Trueblood, *A Place to Stand*.

46 Gilbert W. Stafford, *Theology for Disciples*.

47 George Barna, *America at the Crossroads*.

48 This storybook is Barry L. Callen, *Bible Stories for Strong Stomachs*.

49 Barry L. Callen, *All of God's Word for All of My Needs*, especially the sections "An Earthly King?" "No Compromise!" "Trouble in the Sanctuary!" and "Straying Churches."

50 Kevin W. Mannoia, *Masterful Living.*

51 Barry L. Callen, *Catch Your Breath!*

52 E. Stanley Jones, *Abundant Living.*

53 Barry L. Callen, *Christian Holiness.*

54 My masters thesis at Asbury Theological Seminary was a study in "ecumenical idealism," including the historic relationship between the Church of God (Anderson) and the Free Methodist Church.

55 Barry L. Callen, *Radical Christianity.*

56 Willard Swartley, in Barry L. Callen, *Radical Christianity.*

57 Stanley Hauerwas and William Willimon, *Resident Aliens.*

58 See Donald W. Dayton, *Rediscovering an Evangelical Heritage.*

59 C. Leonard Allen, *Distant Voices, Discovering a Forgotten Past for a Changing Church.*

60 Reported in the autobiography of E. Stanley Jones, *Song of Ascents.*

61 Drawn from Barry L. Callen, *The Prayer of Holiness-Hungry People.*

62 Paraphrase of Eugene Peterson, *The Message.*

63 Kevin W. Mannoia, *The Integrity Factor.*

64 Henry H. Knight III, *Anticipating Heaven Below.*

65 Barry L. Callen, *Approaching Theology.*

66 Thomas Merton, *Thoughts in Solitude.*

67 Benjamin F. Reid, *Glory to the Spirit.*

68 Clark H. Pinnock, *Flame of Love.*

69 Hymn by Martin Luther, *A Mighty Fortress Is Our God.*

70 Henri J. Nouwen, *Out of Solitude.*

71 Hubert Harriman and Barry L. Callen, *Color Me Holy.*

72 Howard A. Snyder, *The Radical Wesley.*

73 Diane Leclerc, in Barry L. Callen and Don Thorsen, *Heart & Life.*

74 Hymn title "Open My Eyes, That I May See" by Clara Scott.

75 Kevin W. Mannoia, "A Case for Engagement."

76 Jonathan S. Raymond, *Social Holiness.*

77 D. Michael Henderson, *John Wesley's Class Meeting.*

78 There is an excellent series of Christian books on reconciliation by Curtiss Paul DeYoung. One, written with his friend George Samuel Hines in 2011, is *Beyond Rhetoric: Reconciliation as a Way of Life*.

79 See the units "Where's the Justice" and "Protecting Faith's Integrity" in Barry L. Callen, *All of God's Word for All of My Needs*.

80 Barry L. Callen, *Authentic Spirituality*.

81 Charles Wesley, "Lost in Wonder, Love, and Praise!"

82 See Barry L. Callen, editor, *The Holy River of God*.

83 Barry L. Callen, *Forward, Ever Forward*! (Church of God Movement, Anderson).

84 Gilbert W. Stafford, in Barry L. Callen and Don Thorsen, *Heart & Life*.

85 Barry L. Callen, *A Pilgrim's Progress*, 4th ed., 2024.

86 See James Earl Massey, *Views from the Mountain*, Select Writings, ed. Barry L. Callen with Curtiss DeYoung. Note my work with a range of other persons well worth remembering, told in my several published biographies and institutional histories. Don't miss *The Wisdom of the Saints*, 2003.

87 Gloria Gaither concerning herself and husband Bill in her book *Because He Lives*.

88 The autobiography of Dag Hammarskjold.

89 From the novel *This Tender Land* by William Kent Krueger.

90 David Elton Trueblood's autobiography is titled *While It Is Day*.

91 Sermon "The Face of Jesus" by James Earl Massey in his *Sundays in the Tuskegee Chapel*.

92 Timothy Johnson, *Finding God in the Questions*.

93 See Barry L. Callen, *Radical Christianity*.

94 The primary pioneer of this reforming movement was Daniel S. Warner. His biography is Barry L. Callen's *It's God's Church!*

95 This book is by James S. Stewart of Edinburgh, Scotland, titled *The Strong Name*.

96 See Barry L. Callen, *Caught Between Truths*.

97 Gilbert W. Stafford, *Theology for Disciples*.

98 Seattle Pacific University, associated with the Free Methodist Church and yet seeking to function for the good of the whole body of Christians.

99 Stanley J. Grenz, *Theology for the Community of God.*

100 For an explanation of how the "Old" Testament should be related to the "New," even calling them the "Foundational" and "Final" Testaments, see Barry L. Callen, *Beneath the Surface*, 2012.

101 Howard A. Snyder, *Homosexuality and the Church*, struggles with the exclusion element of Christian inclusiveness.

102 William O. Cushing's hymn *"Under His Wings."*

103 Most recent of my biographies have been *John S. Pistole* and *Anchored and Reaching* (Kevin W. Mannoia).

104 A comprehensive study of biblical interpretation is Clark H. Pinnock and Barry L. Callen, *The Scripture Principle.*

105 Cheryl Bridges Johns, *Re-enchanting the Text.*

106 Winn Collier, *A Burning in My Bones*, a biography of Eugene H. Peterson.

107 See Barry L. Callen, *Beneath the Surface* and *Bible Stories for Strong Stomachs.*

108 For this plan fully developed, see Barry L. Callen, *All of God's Word for All of My Needs.*

109 Walter Brueggemann, *The Message of the Psalms.*

110 Barry L. Callen, with Kevin Mannoia and Don Thorsen, *Golden Nuggets of Truth.*

111 *Our Great Redeemer's Praise* (2022) features many hymns organized helpfully by the theological elements of the Apostles' Creed.

112 Editors of *A Year with Rabbi Jesus* are Barry Callen, Steve Hoskins, and Jonathan Powers.

113 The full conversation is found in Barry L. Callen, *Heart of the Matter.*

114 Thomas Merton's dramatic life story is told in his autobiography, *The Seven Storey Mountain.*

115 See Roger E. Olson in his internet theological musings, *Patheos*, December 14, 2024.

116 Martin Luther King, Jr., *Letter from the Birmingham Jail.*

117 Composed by Elisha A. Hoffman.

118 James Earl Massey, *Views from the Mountain.* See also Diane Leclerc, *Discovering Christian Holiness,* and Barry L. Callen, *Christian Holiness.*

119 Barry L. Callen, *The Prayer of Holiness-Hungry People.*

120 Mildred Bangs Wynkoop, *A Theology of Love.*

121 Charles Wesley, "The Thing My Lord Doth Hate." See his brother John's *The Character of a Methodist.*

122 This realization is elaborated in the systematic theology of Barry L. Callen titled *God As Loving Grace.*

123 Elaine A. Heath, *Five Means of Grace: Experience God's Love the Wesleyan Way.*

124 Thomas C. Oden, *After Modernity...What?*

125 I titled my history of the United States across the twentieth century *Seeking the Light: America's Modern Quest for Peace, Justice, Prosperity, and Faith.*

126 Barry L. Callen, *Faithful in the Meantime.*

127 Much detail about "modernism" and "post-modernism" is found in Barry L. Callen, *Time To Think Again!*

128 Merle Strege, *I Saw the Church.*

129 Barry L. Callen, *Radical Christianity.*

130 For the history of the visions, achievements, and frustrations of the Church of God Movement, see Barry L. Callen, *Forward, Ever Forward!*

131 These lyrics are by John E. Bode.

132 Barry L. Callen, *Golden Nuggets of Truth.*

133 Sermon of John Wesley, "Walking by Sight and Walking by Faith."

134 Hymn lyrics of "Jesus Calls Us O'er the Tumult" by Cecil Frances Alexander.

135 Hymn lyrics of "Will Your Anchor Hold in the Storms of Life?" by Priscilla J. Owens.

136 Clark H. Pinnock and Barry L. Callen, *The Scripture Principle.*

137 Spiros Zodhiates, *The Lord's Prayer.*

138 See Barry L. Callen, *The Living Dead.*

139 See Barry L. Callen, *The Living Dead.*

140 Lyrics of "Breathe on Me, Breath of God" by Edwin Hatch.

141 Lyrics of "Christ the Lord is Risen Today" by Charles Wesley.

142 Barry L. Callen, *The Jagged Journey*.

143 Jürgen Moltmann, *The Coming of God*.

144 Barry L. Callen, *Faithful in the Meantime*.

145 Hal Lindsey's 1970 book *The Late Great Planet Earth* was a marketplace success. He used this as evidence of its content's correctness.

146 Clark H. Pinnock, in Barry L. Callen, *Heart of the Matter*, and in their joint book, *The Scripture Principle*.

147 Stanley J. Grenz, *The Millennial Maze*.

148 H. Ray Dunning, *Biblical Heights for Today's Valleys*.

149 Barry L. Callen, *Faithful in the Meantime*.

150 Daniel W. Whittle, hymn "I Know Whom I Have Believed."

151 John A. Morrison, *As the River Flows*.

152 This hope is elaborated in Barry L. Callen, *Authentic Spirituality*.

153 Lines from Charles Wesley's hymn "*Come, Let Us Join Our Friends Above.*"

154 Clark H. Pinnock, *Flame of Love*.

155 On salvation for non-Christians, see Randy Maddox, *Responsible Grace*.

156 Barry L. Callen, *The Jagged Journey*.

157 Clark H. Pinnock, *Flame of Love*.

158 Hymn lyrics by Charles Wesley, *Come, Let Us Join Our Friends Above*.

159 Barry L. Callen, *God in the Shadows*.

160 Amos Yong, *Renewing Christian Theology*.

161 Poem by Langston Hughes.

162 Henry H. Knight III, *Anticipating Heaven Below*.

163 Kevin W. Mannoia, *15 Characteristics of Effective Pastors*.

164 Jürgen Moltmann, *In the End—The Beginning*.

165 Verse one of David Elton Trueblood's hymn "*Baptism by Fire.*"

166 Brenna Blain, *Can I Say That?*

167 James Earl Massey, *Sundays in the Tuskegee Chapel*.

168 Barry L. Callen, *A Pilgrim's Progress*, fourth edition, 2024.

www.ingramcontent.com/pod-product-compliance
Lightning Source LLC
Chambersburg PA
CBHW062022220426
43662CB00010B/1440